HE'S GOT YOUR SIX

HEALING THROUGH BIBLICAL PRINCIPLES

John Galanti

Scripture quotations marked CEB are taken from the COMMON ENGLISH BIBLE © Copyright 2011. COMMON ENGLISH BIBLE. All rights reserved. Used by permission. Www.CommonEnglishBible.com.

Scripture quotations marked ESV are taken from the ESV® Bible (The Holy Bible, English Standard Version®), copyright © 2001 by Crossway Bibles, a publishing ministry of Good News Publishers. ©All rights reserved.

Scripture quotations marked NASB1995 are taken from the New American Standard Bible® (NASB), Copyright © 1960, 1962, 1963, 1968, 1971, 1972, 1973, 1975, 1977, 1995 by The Lockman Foundation. Used by permission. www.Lockman.org.

Scripture quotations marked NIV are taken from the Holy Bible, New International Version®, NIV®. Copyright © 1973, 1978, 1984, 2011 by Biblica, Inc.TM Used by permission of Zondervan. All rights reserved worldwide. www.zondervan.com. The "NIV" and "New International Version" are trademarks registered in the United States Patent and Trademark Office by Biblica, Inc.TM

Scripture quotations marked NKJV are taken from the New King James Version®. Copyright © 1982 by Thomas Nelson. Used by permission. All rights reserved.

Scripture quotations marked NLT are taken from the Holy Bible, New Living Translation, copyright © 1996, 2004, 2015 by Tyndale House Foundation. Used by permission of Tyndale House Publishers, Inc., Carol Stream, Illinois 60188. All rights reserved.

Scripture quotations marked TLB are taken from The Living Bible copyright © 1971. Used by permission of Tyndale House Publishers, a Division of Tyndale House Ministries, Carol Stream, Illinois 60188. All rights reserved.

Scripture quotations marked KJV are taken from the King James Version of the Bible. Public domain.

He's Got Your Six
Healing through Biblical Principles
ISBN: 978-1-685730-69-7
Copyright © 2024 by John Galanti

Published by Word and Spirit Publishing
P.O. Box 701403
Tulsa, Oklahoma 74170
wordandspiritpublishing.com

Printed in the United States of America. All rights reserved under International Copyright Law. Content and/or cover may not be reproduced in whole or in part in any form without the expressed written consent of the Publisher.

DEDICATION

I WANT TO DEDICATE THIS BOOK to all the people who helped me find my way. First, my wife, Tina, who is always encouraging and there for me; then, my church and church family; as well as my men's group, Iron Sharpens Iron. I also want to thank Mike Wenell for helping make *HGY6* a reality.

CONTENTS

Introduction vii
1　Why Believe? 1
2　Spiritual Battle: Know Your Enemy 13
3　Healing through Biblical Principles 29
4　Heaven or Hell? 43
5　Promises and Warnings 57
6　Repent or Perish 71
7　The Unlikely Disciples 81
8　Inspiring Thoughts, Writings, and Stories 99
9　The Rapture and Tribulation 121
10　Biblical Principles and Political Policies 135
11　Put in the Work 143

Introduction

SOME OF THE THINGS WRITTEN in this book may be hard to hear, while other things are simply amazing. We seem to be living in a time when many want to avoid tough topics and shy away from many of the warnings that were given in the Bible.

My hope is that this book will open a new way of healing in your life. Where there is hope, there is healing.

I believe we need to understand the promises that Jesus wanted us to know, along with the dire warnings that have been written and prophesied. For us to get the full message that Jesus came to share, we need to be open to *all* the writings in the Bible, not just pick and choose the ones that make us feel good. Unfortunately, we see this in far too many churches and pastor's teachings.

Knowing the attacks and tactics of our enemy prepares us so we do not fall into desperate situations or look for healing in places that will only bring more problems. Many people look to drugs, alcohol, lust, power, possessions, and many other activities for relief, but these just mask our problems and lead to even worse outcomes.

I believe that when we follow the instructions laid out in the Bible, we begin walking the path toward true healing, contentment, and peace. It takes commitment and dedication, but once you make that choice, I know you will find it worth the time you invest.

I am not a pastor, nor do I claim to be a teacher. I am just an average guy who loves the Lord! What I have written is my understanding of the Bible through my daily studies and research. I have no formal education or teaching credentials. But what I do have is the wisdom and discernment God provides me through the Holy Spirit. All I want is to do is His will.

Some people think that because their past is so heinous, God won't forgive them for what they have done. I was one of those people. Now I see the grace of God and understand that God will forgive each of us, no matter what we have done, if we simply reach out to Him.

My past was marked with events that would make anyone think there was no way that God would accept me. But learning what is "actually" written in the Bible made it possible for me to understand how much God loves me and wants me to spend eternity with Him and the Lord Jesus. The same is true for you. If we seek Him, He will welcome us—but only if we truly seek Him in our hearts.

I came to this understanding. Because of free will, each of us has to take that first step! God will accept each of us if we reach out to Him with a true heart and repent of our sins. Jesus paid the price for our sins so that we can have eternal life with our heavenly Father.

The simple message is that we first must believe with our heart that Jesus is our Lord and Savior (the One who offers salvation). Go ahead and do the research like I did, so you can truly believe. Don't take my word for it—learn for yourself what God is offering you and what Jesus' message truly is.

I often say, "It is a simple message, with a lot of detail." You must repent of your sins and ask for forgiveness. This means turning away from your sins. If just being a good person was enough, then Jesus wouldn't have had to suffer death in the most horrendous method imaginable. Crucifixion is the worst method of being put to death. And thinking that you can just be a good person and get into heaven minimizes the sacrifice Jesus made for us.

Each of us has broken God's moral Law, which are comprised of the Ten Commandments. We are all sinners. But Jesus paid our debt in full so that we can have everlasting life.

You must worship God as your one and only God. People worship all kinds of idols. God doesn't want us to go down that path. This is why He requires us to focus on Him—and only Him. It's for our own good. That is how much He loves us. All He really wants is a relationship with us.

My goal in writing this book is to expose you, the reader, to Scripture. I know God's Word brings true healing! This book is also meant to help you start a routine of your own that will lead you to greater understanding of the Word that has been inspired by God for our benefit. If you take the time to commit to forming a daily habit of reading the Bible, the reward will be greater than any other investment you could possibly commit to.

"What good will it be for someone to gain the whole world, yet forfeit their soul? Or what can anyone give in exchange for their soul?"

—Matthew 16:26 NIV

The wages of sin is death, but the gift of God is eternal life.

—Romans 6:23 NIV

"Come to me, all you who are weary and burdened, and I will give you rest. Take my yoke upon you and learn from me, for I am gentle and humble in heart, and you will find rest for your souls. For my yoke is easy and my burden is light."

—Matthew 11:28–30 NIV

Jesus came into our world to show us a better way, a way that leads to life and to contentment.

What Does *"Got Your Six"* Mean?

"Got your six" is a common phrase used in police or military jargon; it means that someone is looking out for your back. The phrase comes from the way airplane pilots used to refer to various directions around themselves as if they stood in the center of a clock: "in front of" became "12 o'clock," while "behind" became "6 o'clock."

When a person is covering someone else's back, they will tell them, "I got your six."

INTRODUCTION

What's the Origin of *"Got Your Six"*?

The origin of this phrase can be traced back to World War 1, when aerial combat was introduced into the vast array of military tactics. Between 1914 and 1918, aviators developed the lingo for these clock-like directions in the sky.

Over the years and throughout the development of aerial warfare, "got your six" became a commonly encountered phrase, spoken by brothers-in-arms who were ready to protect each other from harm.

How Did *"Got Your Six"* Spread?

The phrase "got your six" was eventually adopted by other branches of the military, including infantry and mechanized units, eventually reaching a state of commonness that the expression was endorsed by law enforcement, as well (digitalcultures.net).

I can see how, in human language, the phrase "got your six" was used in battle and protection. But for me, the ultimate Protector is God! There is no other One I would want more to have my back!

1
WHY BELIEVE?

THE FIRST STEP IN HEALING through biblical principles is that you must *believe*. It is literally a matter of life and death: the matter of how and where you spend your life after your physical death. Hopefully, this book helps you find that belief. I hope you will be able to answer the question with certainty if asked, "Do you know if you will go to heaven when you die?"

> ***Jesus said,*** *"I am the way and the truth and the life.* ***No one*** *comes to the Father except through me."*
>
> —John 14:6 NIV, emphasis mine

> Jesus said, *"Very truly I tell you, no one can see the kingdom of God unless they are born again."*
>
> —John 3:3 NIV

If you don't believe in God, or that Jesus is God, or that the written Word is from God, why would you think you will go to heaven? You don't even believe what has been written! It is of the most importance to know the words that God left for us. The *BIBLE* contains *Basic Instructions Before Leaving Earth*. Remember, it is your choice to believe or not to believe, but your decision will have eternal consequences. Only you are responsible for where you spend eternity.

I speak to so many people who claim to be Christians, or who follow some variance of Christianity. Unfortunately, when you ask them even basic questions about the Scriptures, they don't have much, if any, knowledge of what is written. In addition, they don't live the way a true follower of Christ should live. This is why so many people think of Christians as hypocrites—and many are. This should not condemn all Christians; there are hypocrites in every walk of life.

When pressed on whether they are going to heaven when they die, many people just fall back on the answer, "Well, I'm a good person." If you know the Scriptures, you would also know it takes more than just thinking you have good things in your life. We are all sinners who are in need of a Savior. If that wasn't the case, then Jesus would have gone to the cross for no reason. Thinking this way minimizes the sacrifice Jesus made for us.

Jesus suffered the most brutal death. First, He was whipped to the edge of death, to the point that His skin was falling off His body; then He was punched and spit upon. He had a ring of thorns pressed down on His forehead. He then had to drag a heavy cross through the streets while persecuted. This finally ended with Him having His hands and feet nailed to the wooden cross, where He hung until His body drained of all its blood.

I am sorry to be so graphic, but I will not minimize Jesus' sacrifice. Do you find it odd that His last words were *"It is finished"*? What this meant was that *our debt has been paid*; He had defeated the evil one who ruled this world: *"For the wages of sin is death, but the gift of God is eternal life in Christ Jesus our Lord"* (Romans 6:23 NIV). Our debt of sin was paid by a God who loves us.

I hope you catch hold of this next passage. The importance of these words is crucial to how and where you will spend eternity:

> *"The true light that gives light to everyone was coming into the world. He was in the world, and though the world was made through him, the world did not recognize him. He came to that which was his own, but his own did not receive him.* **Yet to all who did receive him, to those who believed in his name, he gave the right to become children of God**—*children born not of natural descent, nor of human decision or of husband's will, but born of God."*
>
> —John 1:9–13 NIV, emphasis mine

To be a child of God, to earn the right to live in His Kingdom, you must first receive Him into your life. You must believe in Him and accept Jesus Christ as your own Lord and Savior. It is of utmost importance that you understand and believe that God came to earth to offer you the opportunity to spend eternity with Him.

I ask you again: Why believe? Your belief is essential to having strong faith, to letting yourself be open to understanding what has been written. There are many facts found in the Bible. And there is also much critical thinking and common sense. It is not a negative response to want to know the facts. God gave us these facts and examples so that our faith would be strong and continue to grow.

Christianity hinges on the resurrection of Jesus, and the facts that support this claim are undeniable. Without the resurrection,

Christianity would not have had a chance to survive the last 2000-plus years.

I love the words spoken in Acts 5:38–39. A Pharisee named Gamaliel, a teacher of the Law, made the following claims to the Sanhedrin about two of the apostles:

"Therefore, in the present case I advise you: Leave these men alone! Let them go! For if their purpose or activity is from human origin, it will fail. But if it is from God, you will not be able to stop these men; you will only find yourselves fighting against God."

Acts 5:40 says that *"his speech persuaded them. They called the apostles in and had them flogged. Then they ordered them not to speak in the name of Jesus, and let them go."*

Now, to set the scene a little. This took place after Jesus' death and resurrection. These men had nothing to gain and everything to lose by sticking with the story that Jesus had come back from the dead and was the long-awaited Messiah.

Flogging is a nicer-sounding word that means "brutally beaten with whips"; these whips had iron and rock tied at the ends that would rip open the victims' skin. I ask, would you stick to a lie under these, and worse, conditions? Early Christians were fed to lions and burned as candles (the term *Roman candle* comes from this practice)—all because they would not deny what Jesus did to secure our salvation.

Satan wants nothing more than for you to brush all this off and discount it as a tall tale or a fantasy story. He certainly doesn't want you to start researching the facts and discovering that what society has been feeding you was nothing but lies. What a tactic!

Other tactics of the devil include working to keep you from opening your heart, seeking God for an understanding of the Word, or asking God for discernment and wisdom when reading His Word. God says, "Ask and you will receive. Knock and I will answer." Do you think the devil wants you to know these words of the Lord?

> "Ask and it will be given to you; seek and you will find; knock and the door will be opened to you. For everyone who asks receives; the one who seeks finds; and to the one who knocks, the door will be opened. Which of you, if your son asks for bread, will give him a stone? Or if he asks for a fish, will give him a snake? If you, then, though you are evil*, know how to give good gifts to your children, how much more will your Father in heaven give good gifts to those who ask him!"
>
> —Matthew 7:7–11 NIV

*The use of the word *evil* in this passage can be interpreted to man having a sinful nature. God has a sinless nature.

Prophecy

This is just another reason *why you should believe*. Explore the predictions of Jesus' birth, the coming of the Messiah, and His death. Isaiah 53 is a great place to start in this regard, then follow that with Isaiah 9. I will leave these for you to look up and read on your own. Many religious leaders who don't believe Jesus was God actually forbid the teaching of these Scriptures. This made me want to read them even more! There is something very special about opening the Bible and asking God for understanding and then reading the words yourself. God's Word will move within you if you let it. You have to ask yourself, "Why are these chapters held back in so many teachings?" Please take the time to read them for yourself.

Here are just a few samples of the prophetic verses from Isaiah; I hope this small taste encourages you to look them all up for yourself and read the before-and-after verses to gain context. Quick note: Isaiah's words were written almost seven hundred years *before* the birth of Jesus. Other prophecies about the Messiah were even older.

For to us a child is born, to us a son is given, and the government will be on his shoulders.

—Isaiah 9:6 NIV

"Therefore the Lord himself will give you a sign: The virgin will conceive and give birth to a son, and will call him Immanuel." Immanuel translated means God with us.

—Isaiah 7:14 NIV

In reference to the healings that took place in the ministry of Jesus, read Isaiah 35:5–6 (NIV):

Then will the eyes of the blind be opened and the ears of the deaf unstopped. Then will the lame leap like deer, and the mute tongue shout for joy.

Jesus would also proclaim the good news to the poor, comfort the brokenhearted, and set the captives free (Isaiah 61:1).

Jesus, though innocent, would die (Isaiah 53:9). He'd be betrayed by a close friend (Psalm 41:9), *"for thirty pieces of silver"* (Zechariah 11:12 NIV).

He was despised and rejected.

—Isaiah 53:3 NIV

He was beaten and spit on (Isaiah 50:6), pierced in both the hands and the feet (Psalm 22:16), and ultimately killed (Daniel 9:26).

Throughout the prophets' writings, we are given glimpses of Jesus' life, death, and resurrection—as well as what is still to come. How can't you believe? The evidence is so overwhelming! I have touched on just a very few of the many prophecies that Jesus fulfilled.

The number of prophecies found in the Bible depends on how you define a *prophecy*. One source counts *1,239 prophecies in the Old Testament and 578 prophecies in the New Testament, for a total of 1,817.* Another source estimates that there were approximately two hundred to four hundred prophecies given in the Old Testament that Jesus fulfilled. The fulfillment of these prophecies is seen as evidence of Jesus being the true Messiah.

The Resurrection

The resurrection is the lynchpin to the entirety of Christianity. As the apostle Paul said, our faith would be "useless," the Gospel would be altogether powerless, and our sins would remain unforgiven without the resurrection of the Lord. Read 1 Corinthians 15:14–19.

The resurrection of Jesus Christ is also important because it validates who Jesus claimed to be: the *Son of God* and *Messiah*. According to Jesus, His resurrection was the "sign from heaven" that authenticated His ministry.

Jesus appeared to His apostles after His death on the cross, thus proving He had been raised from the dead. Read Luke 24:36–49.

Paul talks about further evidence of Jesus' return from the dead after His crucifixion. Read 1 Corinthians 15:3–8.

In the book, and later movie, *A Case for Christ*, author Lee Strobel, originally an atheist, set out to disprove that the resurrection ever happened. He thought he would be able to disprove this in a weekend after learning that his agnostic wife had found Jesus.

Lee was an editor for the *Chicago Tribune*, one of the biggest papers in the 1980s. Familiar with journalistic standards of "evidence" and "facts," Lee ended up spending over two years trying to disprove the resurrection, only to realize the evidence was clearly factual and verifiable through all the known methods of researching historical documents and events.

To this day, Lee is called a Christian apologetic, one who defends the Christian faith. He now works to spread the Good News of our Savior through his many writings and speaking engagements.

Another great resource on the factual nature of the resurrection is a booklet written by Ray Comfort titled *The Facts of the Bible*. Many people have tried to disprove Jesus' claim of being the Son of Man, only to come up short. Even the Harvard Law School undertook a project to try to disprove Jesus' claims, and they came up short. Ironically, in so many instances, those who researched the topic became Christians.

Then there is just plain old common sense—something that is becoming increasingly rare these days. I wrote about this some years ago in my book *Living Life God's Way*. I believe this process helped me so much in my early walk with the Lord—just seven years ago.

The Importance of the Resurrection of Jesus Christ

I offer the following observations concerning the resurrection. These points have provided me with a clear response to give to any nonbeliever on this topic.

Twelve apostles claimed to have seen Jesus after He was raised from the dead, including Paul. Paul, who had been one of the most powerful Pharisees, was also one of the primary persecutors of Christians in the very early days of the Church. But after witnessing the resurrected Christ for himself, he was severely beaten and locked in a prison full of sewage and rats. Even after all the persecution he experienced, he never denied Jesus and His resurrection—even up to the moment of his beheading.

Every one of these disciples experienced extreme persecution. All but one, the apostle John, suffered imprisonment and/or a brutal death. (John was exiled to the island of Patmos and later wrote the book of Revelation.)

Now, if the resurrection had started out as a lie that originated by the followers of Jesus, do you think they would have continued to follow Jesus' teachings? How far do you think a group of common, uneducated followers would be willing to take it? To their death? All of them?

The disciples witnessed their Teacher, Someone they loved, put to a brutal death, tortured, ridiculed, and crucified—a death they surely would not want to endure themselves.

Do you think it is likely that all the apostles—and later countless disciples and followers—would have stuck to this so-called story, a lie that would ensure their death?

This brings me to the topic of human nature—which is essentially self-preservation. I could see maybe one or possibly two disciples continuing the story of the resurrection for their own purposes. But if you think *all eleven and Paul*, along with *so many others*, knowing it was a lie, would stick to the same story after their own persecution, torture, imprisonment, and threats of a brutal death were levied against them, then you might not understand human nature. It would have only taken one of them saying it was a lie to put doubt in people's minds.

The point is, after Jesus was put to death, none of these men had anything to gain from continuing their quest to spread the words of Jesus—and they had everything to lose—yet all of them did just that.

All of them sacrificed everything they had, traveled as far as they could, endured suffering, and wrote the New Testament to share the faith with the world, all in the name of Jesus Christ. They had no motive to continue this narrative—unless the resurrection actually took place.

As J. Warner Wallace has noted in his lectures and books, when a conspiracy is formed, there are three motivating factors behind such a move: power, greed, and/or lust.

The disciples would hold no *power* behind claiming the resurrection as truth. They were often threatened by the Jewish and Roman authorities.

As for *greed*, they taught that people should not desire earthly possessions, but spiritual ones.

Lust was not a factor, either. They taught celibacy before marriage and marital fidelity after marriage.

In fact, N.T. Wright notes in his classic book *The Resurrection of the Son of God* that the disciples had no theological motivation behind claiming that Jesus had risen from the dead, as they were anticipating a military hero and a final resurrection at the end of time.

What motivating factors existed for these disciples to invent such a story? None!

The only reason the disciples taught the resurrection of Jesus was because Jesus' resurrection *had actually occurred*, and *they witnessed it*!

I mentioned the movie *The Case for Christ* earlier. Again, I suggest watching this movie and seeing for yourself the evidence Lee Strobel of the *Chicago Tribune* uncovered while trying to disprove the resurrection—only to realize that the evidence for the event is overwhelming.

As C.S. Lewis once said: "Christianity, if false, is of no importance, and if true, of infinite importance. The only thing it cannot be is moderately important."

Why did the apostles persist in their beliefs? Could it be that they had truly witnessed God on earth and they understood that Jesus was offering us all eternal life? Only something of the magnitude of the resurrection of Jesus Christ would cause them to be willing to continue to do what they did.

My last point is this: If, knowing this, you still do not want to learn more of what Jesus was trying to tell us, then I just don't understand what it would take.

My prayer is that you understand that *God's Got Your Six*, and that He would reveal the truth to you and all who read this book.

2

Spiritual Battle: Know Your Enemy

SOLDIERS TRAIN TO KNOW THEIR enemies: their strengths, their weaknesses, and the tactics they follow so they can be prepared to face those enemies and ultimately defeat them in battle. They train for all possible scenarios. It is not only soldiers who train and prepare; we all do. Throughout life, we train for our careers, to get a good education, to be great at a sport, to become an entertainer, and many other purposeful life activities. All these activities require hard work, dedication, and commitment.

Unfortunately, most people never train or prepare for the battle against their spiritual enemy. To experience a true relationship with God and healing for addiction, PTSD, anxiety, depression, or any other life problem you are going through, you first must prepare yourself with the tools God offers us—His spiritual armor. You must also know the warnings, along with the promises He shares with us through His written Word (the Bible).

There is a spiritual battle going on for our souls. Many of the problems we are facing in this life are because of this battle. The Bible addresses the way to handle every situation we encounter in this lifetime.

There is good and evil. This is pointed out throughout both the Old Testament and the New Testament. Our spiritual readiness will determine how and where we spend eternity and how we navigate through this life! Can there be anything more important than that?

We've been conditioned to put so much emphasis on worldly events, possessions, and planning for our future on this earth while we are alive, but increasingly many are not putting the same emphasis on what was promised and warned about once we pass away from this earth.

Who is this enemy of your soul? The Bible spells it out very clearly. Below are just a few passages that answer this question:

> *Stay alert! Watch out for your great enemy, the devil. He prowls around like a roaring lion, looking for someone to devour.*
>
> —1 Peter 5:8 NLT

> *"The thief comes only to steal and kill and destroy; I have come that they may have life, and have it to the full."*
>
> —John 10:10 NIV

> *For we are not fighting against flesh-and-blood enemies, but against evil rulers and authorities of the unseen world, against mighty powers in this dark world, and against evil spirits in the heavenly places.*
>
> —Ephesians 6:12 NLT

SPIRITUAL BATTLE: KNOW YOUR ENEMY

Satan's goal is to separate us from God. If he is successful, this will have consequences that will last for eternity.

The good news is that we have God on our side.

If you are paying any attention at all, it is very easy to see that we are in a spiritual battle. Let's break down just these three warnings above. There are many others, but I wanted to point out just three of them for now:

1 Peter 5:8

From the verse above, the very first instruction is to *stay alert*!

The tactic of our enemy is to keep us distracted, to shift our focus to something else through tactics like division, doubt, hate, deceit, and confusion. We see many more tactics hurled at us daily—and they seem to be coming at an alarming rate lately. Could this be because Satan is becoming increasingly desperate? His time is running out, just as the Bible predicted (prophesied)! We remain alert by staying in the Word so we can recognize the schemes of the evil spirits sent to attack us.

Next in 1 Peter 5:8, we are given a description and a dire warning. This is like intel; the Bible is letting us know what our enemy wants to do and how he intends to do it.

If I was in a parking lot and I received a warning that there was a lion prowling around the area, and the person who gave me the warning said the lion wanted to devour anything in its sight, I know I would heed the warning. If I had my family and my kids with me, I guarantee you I would make sure they were all well aware of the threat!

Tell me why people do not heed the warning that the enemy could devour us, our families, and our children for eternity. Do you understand the importance of this warning? I know one reason: Most people don't know God's Word. They don't take the time to train or to understand. I see so many people who have bought into another tactic of the enemy. People ask them, "How can you believe the Bible?" or they tell them it was written so long ago, and it was just a bunch of stories that have been passed down through the generations. What an effective tactic, to minimize the warning and put doubt into your opponent.

John 10:10

In these words of Jesus, we not only receive a warning about the enemy, but we are also given such an amazing promise! I absolutely love this passage from the gospel of the Apostle John.

If a thief was in your neighborhood and you had intel that this thief wanted to steal your possessions, and in addition you heard that in other houses in the area he has killed his targets and *destroyed* everything that remained, wouldn't you heed that warning? I can't emphasize enough that God has given us these warnings for a reason. He wants us to know what is happening so we can prepare. The one caveat is that because of free will, it is up to us to study these warnings and to abide in His Word.

James 2:19 (NIV) says, *"You believe that there is one God. Good! Even the demons believe that—and shudder."* Just believing is not enough!

The point is, you can believe, and you can even memorize God's Word, but in your heart, you have to surrender to God, repent (turn away from your sins), ask for forgiveness, and abide in His Word. All of these things are important!

Next, we get an amazing promise. God who came to earth in the human form, Jesus, tells us, *"I have come that they may have life, and have it to the full"* (John 10:10 NIV). In this world, it is not guaranteed that this promise will be fulfilled. It is possible, but more importantly, we are offered eternal life from a God who loves us so much that He sacrificed everything for us.

Ephesians 6:12

This brings me to the most direct, and most frightening, intel I believe we are given. The words of Ephesians 6:12 sound more like the script of a horror movie than a passage out of the Bible. This verse tells us that our enemy is not of this world—"flesh and blood"—but we are in a battle against evil rulers and authorities of the unseen world, a dark world. This should wake up everyone once they read it!

You can try to discount it, but if you have ever seen evil up close, even in a small way, you know it exists. Without God's protection, we will lose this battle against evil, and we will lose the war. That verse finishes with these words: "these are evil spirits in the heavenly places." That means they reside in the spiritual realm. This war is going on all around us, just waiting for us to fail so the devil can achieve his goal of hurting God. His goal is to steal our souls because he knows this is the best weapon he has to hurt God. We all have free will, and the devil knows this. He knows this weakness. Don't let him take that control.

> *What shall we then say to these things? If God be for us, who can be against us?*
>
> —Romans 8:31 KJV

> *"No weapon forged against you will prevail, and you will refute every tongue that accuses you. This is the heritage of the servants of the LORD, and this is their vindication from me," declares the LORD.*
>
> —Isaiah 54:17 NIV

God has our six! He has our back! All we have to do is accept His offer.

Now, here is how the Bible tells us to prepare for battle. How great is this!? Not only does the Bible let us know what we are up against, but it lets us know how to be protected and win the victory.

Get Equipped for the Daily Battles

> *Therefore, put on every piece of God's armor so you will be able to resist the enemy in the time of evil. Then after the battle you will still be standing firm. Stand your ground, putting on the belt of truth and the body armor of God's righteousness. For shoes, put on the peace that comes from the Good News so that you will be fully prepared. In addition to all of these, hold up the shield of faith to stop the fiery arrows of the devil. Put on salvation as your helmet, and take the sword of the Spirit, which is the word of God.*
>
> —Ephesians 6:13–17 NLT

Put on your armor (also known as the believer's armor).

SPIRITUAL BATTLE: KNOW YOUR ENEMY

#1 The Belt of Truth

A soldier is only ready for battle when he is girded with his belt. A Roman soldier's belt was made of metal and thick heavy leather, and it was where he carried his sword. It also had a protective piece that hung down in the front. His belt held all the other pieces of his armor together. To be fitted with his belt meant he was ready to face action.

Truth is the belt that holds the believer's armor together, as well. Ultimate Truth can be found in God's Word and in the Person of Jesus Christ (John 14:6). We must know this Truth in order to protect ourselves against our flesh, the world, and the father of lies. Truth grounds us and reminds us of our identity in Christ.

HOW TO USE THE BELT OF TRUTH

> **Start your day in the Word.** Starting your day the right way is vital to winning the daily battles you will inevitably face. Before anyone else wakes up, set aside at least ten minutes to begin your day in the Word. It is important to immerse yourself in Scripture without distraction.
>
> **End your day in the Word.** In a quiet place before you lie down to sleep at night, dedicate twenty minutes to studying the Word. The *ESV Study Bible* is widely considered one of the best, and it is also the most affordable of the study Bibles.

#2 The Breastplate of Righteousness

The Roman soldier was always equipped with a breastplate. This piece of armor protected his vital organs in the heat of battle—when he wasn't quick enough to take up his shield. The breastplate was protection against the quick and unexpected advances of the enemy.

As believers, we have no righteousness apart from that which has been given to us by Christ. Our breastplate is His righteousness, and His righteousness will never fail. Though we have no righteousness of our own, we must still, by His power, choose to do right. Living a right life, rooted in God's Word, is a powerful way to protect our hearts, kill our flesh, and defeat the enemy.

HOW TO USE THE BREASTPLATE OF RIGHTEOUSNESS

Identify righteous activities in your life that strengthen you. This may be as simple being kind and helpful to others.

Identify unrighteous activities in your life that weaken you. For each of us, this will be unique. Be cautious of watching movies and TV shows that are not aligned with Jesus' teachings. By intentionally exposing yourself to immoral behavior, you are allowing Satan to weaken the walls of protection that Christ is building around you.

#3 Sandals with the Gospel of Peace

A Roman soldier's feet were fitted with sandals called *caligae*. These sandals were made to help protect soldiers' feet during their long marches into battle. The shoes had extremely thick soles and wrapped perfectly around their ankles in a way that protected against blistering. *Caligae* also had spikes on the bottom to help their feet to grip the ground as they traveled. This helped them have a firm foundation.

Believers also have a firm foundation in the Gospel. As believers, we have peace in knowing we are secure in what Jesus has done for us.

HOW TO USE THE GOSPEL OF PEACE

Preach the Gospel to yourself daily.

Remind yourself of the hope you have in Jesus Christ. Because of His sacrifice and your belief in Him, you shall not perish, but have eternal life. Do not wait until the hardship comes to remind yourself of this. Build your foundation on a daily reminder of this hope, and you will be able to get through anything.

Share your testimonies with others.

The easiest and most effective way to share the Gospel with others is to tell the story of how Jesus changed your life.

Be a living example.

The way you walk through life will be seen by many. When you carry yourself with the fruit of the Spirit, people will stop and notice.

#4 The Shield of Faith

The Roman soldier's shield was a complex piece of armor. The shield, also called a *scutum*, was a soldier's primary defensive weapon. It was made of impenetrable wood, leather, canvas, and metal, and it could be doused in water to extinguish the fiery arrows of the enemy.

Faith is the shield of the believer. Trusting in God's power and protection is imperative in remaining steadfast. When the battle rages, we must remember that God works all things for our good. He is always true to His promises.

HOW TO USE THE SHIELD OF FAITH

Take time to remember the promises of God.

When fiery darts try to impact your heart, extinguish them with reminders of God's goodness over your circumstances. Here are some of His promises:

He will never forsake you (Deuteronomy 31:6).

He will meet all your needs (Philippians 4:19).

Call on Him, and He will answer (Psalm 50:10).

He will make your path straight (Proverbs 3:5–6).

A soldier's shield was strongest when linked with another's.

Band together with other believers in the fight of faith. The best way to do this is through the closeness of a small group. This is how the Church began in the first century, and this is where the strongest spiritual bonds are made today.

Recount God's past victories in your life.

Make a list of all the ways God has come through for you in the past. Whenever your faith wavers, recite this list and remember in detail how God made a way where there seemed to be no way.

#5 Helmet of Salvation

The soldier's head is one of his most vulnerable areas. Without his helmet, one blow to the head would prove fatal. The Roman soldier's helmet covered his entire head, facial area, and between the eyes. The rest of the armor would prove useless if he wasn't equipped with the helmet.

The believer's helmet of salvation is the most crucial piece of armor for the Christian. Without the indwelling Holy Spirit, who enters a believer at the moment of salvation, all other armor is useless. Salvation empowers believers to fight. It protects us in our weaknesses. Without salvation, there is no victory.

HOW TO USE THE HELMET OF SALVATION

Stand on the conviction of your salvation.

When you know without a doubt that you are going to heaven because of what Christ did on the cross, not even death can defeat you. We will all face extremely dark times. In these times, our salvation will light the way and carry us home.

Place your thoughts on things above by listening to sermons via podcast.

Be intentional about feeding your mind with spiritual food throughout the day. Load up your podcast library with sermons from the greatest preachers in the world. Play those podcasts every day on the way to and from work, while running errands, or wherever else you go.

#6 The Sword of the Spirit

All other pieces of the soldier's arsenal are defensive weapons, but not his sword. The sword, the *gladius*, was a deadly weapon. In the hands of a skilled warrior, it could pierce through even the strongest armor.

Our sword is the Word of God and the example of Jesus. Every other piece of armor protects us against attacks. With God's Word, we are truly able to go on the offensive to fight and defeat all enemies. Christ used Scripture to defeat Satan when He was tempted in the desert. We must do the same.

HOW TO USE SWORD OF THE SPIRIT

Arm yourself.

Be intentional about reading Scripture. Find a time you can dedicate to reading and studying the Word of God where you are free of distractions.

When attacked, fight back with the Word of God.

When Satan attacked Christ in the desert, He told the enemy, "No . . . for it is written . . ." Use Christ's example when Satan tries to come after you.

When beaten down, immerse yourself in the Bible.

Even those with great faith will have days when they feel like they are barely hanging on. On these days, ten minutes of time in the Word is just not enough. Take a sick day and immerse yourself in His Word for the entire day. Read, study, pray, and repeat.

SPIRITUAL BATTLE: KNOW YOUR ENEMY

#7 Prayer

In prayer, we show our reliance upon God to act and move. Our entire armor is rooted in His strength. Without His presence, we are powerless in the fight. We must fight on our knees. The One who has won the war is with us in the battle. We will see the victory when we fight in His power.

HOW TO USE PRAYER

Pray when your eyes open every morning.

Before you do anything else, go straight into prayer. Start every day asking God for the wisdom to make good decisions, the discipline to stay true to His Word, and the vision to hear His voice for direction.

Pray impulsively throughout the day.

Sometimes we can get caught up in saying the same prayer over and over again. This can lead us to be in autopilot when we are speaking to our Father, to Jesus, and to the Holy Spirit. You can break through the repetition by impulsively praying throughout the day. Pray for the people you encounter. Pray for the people you read about. Pray to express your thanks for the wonder and beauty of God's creation.

Have a conversation with God on your knees before you go to sleep.

There is something powerful about getting on your knees to honor the King of kings. The Creator of it all is omnipresent and available to talk to you at all times. Tell Him what you are thankful for and talk with Him about whatever is on your mind.

Although the war has been won, the daily battle must be fought. Thankfully, we know with every fight we face that we have the armor and weapons to help us defeat the enemy.

It is not just the Good News; it is the Great News!

God wins! **Revelation** is a book of hope and love! It is God's final warning; He doesn't want a single one of His children to perish. The Shepherd leaves the ninety-nine to rescue the one lost sheep (Matthew 18:12–14)—so much so that He gave His only Son. But He also gave us free will. He only wants those who *want* to spend eternity with Him. God won't force us to choose Him, but He will guide us if we stay in relationship with Him, repent, turn from our sins, and love the Lord Jesus.

This is what we are told in **James 4:8 (NKJV)**: *"Draw near to God and He will draw near to you."* But we must take the first action first! *Do not be lukewarm.* This was the warning to the seventh church of Laodicea in Revelation. Laodicea is thought to symbolize the Church age in which we are living today. Any church that does not teach repentance or that teaches that everyone is accepted regardless of their sin is engaged in dangerous teachings; it is leading people astray from the true message found in the Bible. You cannot be an unrepentant sinner and be accepted in the Kingdom of God.

God's Word is your weapon, and training is the key. You need to abide by His every word and be obedient to it. If you do these things, the Holy Spirit will be with you and provide the contentment you long for so much long.

How can you expect to win the biggest battle of your life without any training? Would you expect to be a great soldier or great at a sport, a job, raising a family, or just about any other worldly thing without effort and training? No? Then, why would you expect to overcome the evil that surrounds us daily without knowledge and training? It takes effort!

Do you think you can do this without training in the Word of God? Without being in a daily relationship with Him, or without doing what He has asked you to do? You can't! Evil will creep into your life, mostly in very subtle ways. This is why God gave us the tools to defeat evil. The rest is up to us.

We all know evil is out there; we've all seen it. I've seen it in drug addiction, alcoholism, at work, in boardrooms, in families, and in neighborhoods. It is in every aspect of our lives. But guess what? So is God's love. The good news is, God is more powerful. God is in every aspect of our lives. When we draw near to Him, invite Him into our lives, and understand the Word, only then can we live according to it.

If we stay in a daily relationship with Him, He will give us the strength we need. If not, we will stray! Evil counts on us straying. If we stay in relationship with God and in the Word, we will have His protection from the evil around us. This is His promise to us.

How Do We Stay Ready for the Daily Battle?

The answer to this question is simple: Read the training manual—God's words to us, the **Bible**...

B: Basic

I: Instructions

B: Before

L: Leaving

E: Earth

3

HEALING THROUGH BIBLICAL PRINCIPLES

YOU FIRST MUST KNOW WHAT you are up against before you can ever begin to start to address the pain, the suffering, and the darkness many people feel.

Those who are paying attention can feel that something is not right. They want contentment, they want peace, and they want joy in their lives. Unfortunately, so many people don't want to even try to do what is necessary to achieve this peace. Others don't know where to begin. I hope this book changes that.

The very first thing you should do is ask for help, invite God and Jesus in, then believe that the promises in the Bible are true. Here are six ways to get started.

1. **First, you must believe and invite God into your life. Commit your life to following Jesus each day the best you know how for the rest of your life.**

Repeat these words to God and to Jesus. You must truly mean them in your heart!

Dear Lord,

I admit I am a sinner. I have done many things that does not please You. I have lived my life for myself only. I am sorry, and I repent. I ask You to forgive me. I accept You as my Lord and Savior. I believe that You died on the cross for me, to save me. You did what I could not do for myself. I come to You now and ask You to take control of my life; I give it to You and surrender. From this day forward, help me to live every day for You in a way that pleases You.

I love You, Lord, and I thank You for the opportunity to spend eternity with You.

Amen.

James 4:7–8 (NLT) says, "*So humble yourselves before God. Resist the devil, and he will flee from you. Come close to God, and God will come close to you.*" Because God gave us free will, we must take the first step. Once we submit to His will, He will honor His promises.

2. **Pray.**

Go to a private place every day and pray, even if it is just for a few minutes. Reach out to God. It is as simple as having a conversation with Him. He already knows your thoughts. Just be honest. By doing this daily, you are creating a habit and showing your commitment!

3. **Read the Bible.**

   Study and apply the Word of God. Start reading the Bible every morning. Even if it's just one verse, open the Bible and ask God for understanding! I suggest reading the gospel of John and the book of James first. This is a great start.

   Download the <u>Bible App</u> and listen to the verse of the day.

4. **Attend a Bible-teaching church.**

   My family and I attend Calvary Church here in Jupiter, Florida. There are many Calvary churches throughout the country, and they are known for focusing on the Word.

5. **Join a small group or Bible study.**

   We are all in different stages of our journey with Jesus, but we are not meant to go into battle alone. Join a group of believers with whom you will commit to being open and honest. This is key to your growth and learning how to combat the attacks of the enemy.

6. **Change what you are watching and listening to.**

   Garbage In = Garbage Out.

   Limit social media and change the media to which you are subscribing. I have taken most social media apps off my phone. When I want to check them, I go to my laptop, and that is mainly for work purposes. This helps to rid me of the unhealthy addiction of constantly looking at my phone and missing out on life—the life God gave me. The same holds true for you.

Watch <u>The Case for Christ</u>. This movie is based on a true story. Knowing the facts of the resurrection will help lead you to greater faith and belief in the Lord. In addition, download <u>The Chosen app</u> or stream it and start watching. The available four seasons bring Jesus' story to life. This is a good start. Begin looking for additional programs, podcasts, and videos that will add to your spiritual life.

Don't be concerned about what other people think of you wanting to learn more about Jesus and God—you are doing this for you! Start with some simple changes in your day, and your life will have amazing and positive results.

I absolutely love what Jesus told people in the Bible when He healed them. After curing them of maladies like blindness, deafness, leprosy, crippled limbs, or other diseases,He told them, "Your faith has healed you." He asked them things such as, "Do you believe you can be healed" (by Him)? If we have faith, God will do amazing things in our lives. They may not be on our time schedule, but He will provide peace even in our suffering, and in some instances, He will even heal us physically. More importantly, He heals us mentally and spiritually. He gives us the peace of knowing our suffering is temporary and that we will live forever in His Kingdom once we pass from death to life.

In John 16:33 (NIV, my emphasis), Jesus said, *"I have told you these things, so that in me you may have peace. In this world you **will** have trouble. But take heart! I have overcome the world."*

Sometimes in this world, the cross we must bear is immense, but knowing it is temporary rather than what happens when we are an unrepentant sinner is worth the anguish. It may seem too much to turn from, or it might seem difficult to resist the temptation of the sin in which you are living, but knowing the price we will pay void of God for eternity helps us realize that it is not worth living that sinful life. We have free will, so we do have that choice.

In Matthew 10:28 (NIV), Jesus said, *"Do not be afraid of those who kill the body but cannot kill the soul. Rather, be afraid of the One who can destroy both soul and body in hell."*

I also love the promise Jesus gave us to get through these times so much I had to repeat it:

"Come to me, all you who are weary and burdened, and I will give you rest. Take my yoke upon you and learn from me, for I am gentle and humble in heart, and you will find rest for your souls."

—Matthew 11:28–29 NIV

When I was bound up with conflict within me, this verse gave me new life. I personally understand the effect it has when you truly surrender yourself and abide in God and His Word.

Healing through the Holy Spirit

I believe the Holy Spirit who was promised to us provides healing that we could never imagine. I often say, "If only a non-believer could understand or experience the feeling of the Holy Spirit within them, they would be a believer." The problem is, you must be a believer first, surrendering to God and accepting Jesus as your Lord and Savior. Do you see the dilemma?

God dwells in us if we do what He asks of us. Picture the following! Jesus is sitting on the couch with you. He is in that business meeting with you. He is there when you are all alone. He knows every thought, everything you watch, and everything you are thinking. We are the temple of the Holy Spirit. Knowing the Holy Spirit is with us all the time, we should be much more cautious of our conduct and the content to which we expose ourselves. The good news is, the Holy Spirit is in all of us, and He is there to guide us, if we choose.

If you turn from your sins, repent, and ask Jesus to come into your life, He will fill you with His Spirit—God's Spirit. Every morning, I ask for His Spirit to be renewed in me and to be a light that shines for others to see. Surrender and humble yourself, and all the promises God has offered will be given to you. You must turn from your sins, or you risk being devoured by the roaring lion that seeks to kill and destroy your soul and your spirit.

Throughout the Bible, we are promised that the Holy Spirit will be in us. We are the temple for God's Spirit. Whatever happens during our short time on this planet, how we proceed with the choice of having or not having the Holy Spirit guide us, is of the most importance. Your eternity is riding on it! (Google Pastor Francis Chan's "The Rope.")

In the Lord's Prayer, we have been told to pray, "Your will be done" (Matthew 6:10 NIV)—God's will, not our own! We may not always understand God's will for us, and that's okay, but no matter what the situation is, we must always trust Him. That's faith!

The Holy Spirit is mentioned 766 times in Scripture in one form or another. Do we give the Holy Spirit enough of our attention? The Bible sure did! I don't believe we recognize the Holy Spirit enough or the significance of what God has given us. I can only imagine as the apostles were sitting in that Upper Room, waiting for something but not understanding what it was. Now I know! It was and is the Holy Spirit, but do we really appreciate it?

I once read a book called *The Forgotten God* by Francis Chan. It is amazing and made me aware so much more of the Holy Spirit—aware of how I interact with Him, rely on Him, and trust Him in all situations. Francis points out how important this topic is, but it gets very little attention in most churches. He also points out that the early Christ followers preached mostly about the Holy Spirit.

No matter what has happened in my past, no matter what trials or tragedies I have been through, I am now aware these are all temporary things. The Bible tells us things will get worse. This is what is written. Knowing I have God living in me; knowing I am a citizen of heaven; knowing that once my mission is done on earth, God will take me home—all these things bring me peace, joy, and contentment. Nothing on this earth can take that away from me.

Do you embrace God's mission for your life no matter what, or do you try to do it your way? God's will must be done. Here are forty-one verses that speak about the Holy Spirit. It seems to be a very important message that God wants us to know:

1. "Now the Lord is the Spirit, and where the Spirit of the Lord is, there is freedom" (2 Corinthians 3:17 NIV).

2. "May the God of hope fill you with all joy and peace as you trust in him, so that you may overflow with hope by the power of the Holy Spirit" (Romans 15:13 NIV).

3. "Do you not know that your bodies are temples of the Holy Spirit, who is in you, whom you have received from God? You are not your own; you were bought at a price. Therefore honor God with your bodies" (1 Corinthians 6:19–20 NIV).

4. "And I will ask the Father, and he will give you another advocate to help you and be with you forever" (John 14:16 NIV; be sure to read the rest of the chapter!).

5. "But the Advocate, the Holy Spirit, whom the Father will send in my name, will teach you all things and will remind you of everything I have said to you" (John 14:26 NIV).

6. "Don't you know that you yourselves are God's temple and that God's Spirit dwells in your midst?" (1 Corinthians 3:16 NIV).

7. "They saw what seemed to be tongues of fire that separated and came to rest on each of them. All of them were filled with the Holy Spirit and began to speak in other tongues as the Spirit enabled them" (Acts 2:3–4 NIV; be sure to read the lead-up to these verses).

8. "And hope does not put us to shame, because God's love has been poured out into our hearts through the Holy Spirit, who has been given to us" (Romans 5:5 NIV).

9. "If you then, though you are evil, know how to give good gifts to your children, how much more will your Father in heaven give the Holy Spirit to those who ask him!" (Luke 11:13 NIV).

10. "And do not grieve the Holy Spirit of God, with whom you were sealed for the day of redemption" (Ephesians 4:30 NIV).

11. "But you will receive power when the Holy Spirit comes on you; and you will be my witnesses in Jerusalem, and in all Judea and Samaria, and to the ends of the earth" (Acts 1:8 NIV).

12. "After they prayed, the place where they were meeting was shaken. And they were all filled with the Holy Spirit and spoke the word of God boldly" (Acts 4:31 NIV). Can you imagine what they thought? They had no idea what they were waiting for!

13. "Therefore go and make disciples of all nations, baptizing them in the name of the Father and of the Son and of the Holy Spirit, and teaching them to obey everything I have commanded you. And surely I am with you always, to the very end of the age" (Matthew 28:19–20 NIV).

14. "But you, dear friends, by building yourselves up in your most holy faith and praying in the Holy Spirit, keep yourselves in God's love as you wait for the mercy of our Lord Jesus Christ to bring you to eternal life" (Jude 1:20–21 NIV).

15. "And I will put my Spirit in you and move you to follow my decrees and be careful to keep my laws" (Ezekiel 36:27 NIV).

16. "For who knows a person's thoughts except their own spirit within them? In the same way no one knows the thoughts of God except the Spirit of God" (1 Corinthians 2:11 NIV).

17. "Peter replied, 'Repent and be baptized, every one of you, in the name of Jesus Christ for the forgiveness of your sins. And you will receive the gift of the Holy Spirit'" (Acts 2:38 NIV).

18. "Teach me to do your will, for you are my God; may your good Spirit lead me on level ground" (Psalm 143:10 NIV).

19. "We are witnesses of these things, and so is the Holy Spirit, whom God has given to those who obey him" (Acts 5:32 NIV).

20. "When the Advocate comes, whom I will send to you from the Father—the Spirit of truth who goes out from the Father—he will testify about me" (John 15:26 NIV).

21. "Whenever you are arrested and brought to trial, do not worry beforehand about what to say. Just say whatever is given you at the time, for it is not you speaking, but the Holy Spirit" (Mark 13:11 NIV).

22. "May the grace of the Lord Jesus Christ, and the love of God, and the fellowship of the Holy Spirit be with you all" (2 Corinthians 13:14 NIV).

23. "On hearing this, they were baptized in the name of the Lord Jesus. When Paul placed his hands on them, the Holy Spirit came on them, and they spoke in tongues and prophesied" (Acts 19:5–6 NIV).

24. "While they were worshiping the Lord and fasting, the Holy Spirit said, "Set apart for me Barnabas and Saul for the work to which I have called them" (Acts 13:2 NIV).

25. "For prophecy never had its origin in the human will, but prophets, though human, spoke from God as they were carried along by the Holy Spirit" (2 Peter 1:21 NIV).

26. "When all the people were being baptized, Jesus was baptized too. And as he was praying, heaven was opened and the Holy Spirit descended on him in bodily form like a dove. And a voice came from heaven: 'You are my Son, whom I love; with you I am well pleased'" (Luke 3:21–22 NIV).

27. "This is the word of the LORD to Zerubbabel: 'Not by might nor by power, but by my Spirit,' says the LORD Almighty" (Zechariah 4:6 NIV).

28. "The Spirit of the Sovereign LORD is on me, because the LORD has anointed me to proclaim good news to the poor. He has sent me to bind up the brokenhearted, to proclaim freedom for the captives and release from darkness for the prisoners" (Isaiah 61:1 NIV).

29. "Where can I go from your Spirit? Where can I flee from your presence? If I go up to the heavens, you are there; if I make my bed in the depths, you are there" (Psalm 139:7–8 NIV).

30. And I myself did not know him, but the one who sent me to baptize with water told me, 'The man on whom you see the Spirit come down and remain is the one who will baptize with the Holy Spirit'" (John 1:33 NIV).

31. "But after he had considered this, an angel of the Lord appeared to him in a dream and said, 'Joseph son of David, do not be afraid to take Mary home as your wife, because

what is conceived in her is from the Holy Spirit'" (Matthew 1:20 NIV).

32. "He saved us, not because of righteous things we had done, but because of his mercy. He saved us through the washing of rebirth and renewal by the Holy Spirit" (Titus 3:5 NIV).

33. "As I began to speak, the Holy Spirit came on them as he had come on us at the beginning" (Acts 11:15 NIV).

34. "Surely no one can stand in the way of their being baptized with water. They have received the Holy Spirit just as we have" (Acts 10:47 NIV).

35. "Anyone who speaks a word against the Son of Man will be forgiven, but anyone who speaks against the Holy Spirit will not be forgiven, either in this age or in the age to come" (Matthew 12:32 NIV).

36. "In the beginning God created the heavens and the earth. Now the earth was formless and empty, darkness was over the surface of the deep, and the Spirit of God was hovering over the waters" (Genesis 1:1–2 NIV).

37. "The angel answered, 'The Holy Spirit will come on you, and the power of the Most High will overshadow you. So the holy one to be born will be called the Son of God'" (Luke 1:35 NIV).

38. "And so I tell you, every kind of sin and slander can be forgiven, but blasphemy against the Spirit will not be forgiven" (Matthew 12:31 NIV).

39. "Exalted to the right hand of God, he has received from the Father the promised Holy Spirit and has poured out what you now see and hear" (Acts 2:33 NIV).

40. "Then the church throughout Judea, Galilee and Samaria enjoyed a time of peace and was strengthened. Living in the fear of the Lord and encouraged by the Holy Spirit, it increased in numbers" (Acts 9:31 NIV).

41. "This is how the birth of Jesus the Messiah came about: His mother Mary was pledged to be married to Joseph, but before they came together, she was found to be pregnant through the Holy Spirit" (Matthew 1:18 NIV).

As you can see, the Bible makes it abundantly clear the importance of the Holy Spirit. Once you have accepted Jesus, you will start seeking help in the right places.

Unfortunately, many of us have sought comfort in all the wrong places. If you are like I was, you tried to heal and hide through all the worldly vices, like drinking, drugs, sex, greed, coveting, power, and all the other things that only lead to addictions, emptiness, depression, anxiety, and despair.

Follow Jesus, not the world's temptations and tactics the enemy hopes to use to destroy you. To find true comfort, healing, and contentment, please seek out what God has given to us, His Word.

4

Heaven or Hell?

NOW THINGS ARE ABOUT TO get real!

I was the type who didn't have much fear. I have done some pretty crazy things in my life. Now I wish I'd had more fear back then. I would have probably gotten in less trouble!

I had a vivid dream a short time ago that showed me what true fear is. I was in a building, and I heard a man screaming, "Where are my kids?" When I went to help, he said, "They just disappeared!" Instantly my thoughts went to the Rapture, and I thought that I had been left behind! I have never felt fear anywhere close to that disparaging feeling I had in that dream. In the next seconds, the man's kids ran into the room, and I realized God had not yet taken His Church, and at that moment I woke up. I knew right away what true fear was. It is being separated from God and being left behind to face the tribulation that is to come after the Rapture of God's Church.

Fear can be a very bad thing, but it can also be your best friend. You would not jump out of a plane at 10,000 feet without a parachute for fear of dying. The fear of God is similar. It is the fear of dying, or living a life absent of God for eternity.

When I started to truly understand what heaven and hell really are, the way they are described in the Bible, the way Jesus told us about the realities of them both, I began to understand fear like never before. The fear of being separated from God—the fear of spending eternity in the absence of everything good, absent of love, laughter, friendship, peace, light, and so much more—surely changed my mindset.

I also started to research stories of people who have had Near Death Experiences (NDAs). Some were beyond beautiful; the descriptions were beyond what our minds can comprehend. It has been said that we don't have words even to relate to the experiences God has waiting for us. Then there were those stories that went the other direction; each person's descriptions are eerily similar, and they align with the description of hell in the Bible.

I will try to point out the descriptions of both destinations in this chapter. When someone says to me, "I have good news and bad news. Which do you want to hear first?" I always choose the bad news first, in the hope that the good news will help me recover afterward from hearing the bad news.

I'm going to follow that same pattern and start with the bad news first here in this chapter. Knowing what I know now about both options, it breaks my heart when I hear someone say, "I'm going to hell," even if they are joking! Man, do they really know what they are saying? I love them too much to laugh it off or go along with it without reaching out in some way to help them understand what they are saying. Our eternal destination is serious stuff, and I hope everyone can grasp the levity of our actions. They have extremely detrimental eternal consequences, or they can have amazing eternal rewards. Again, free will dictates which it will be for all of us.

I heard this said once and thought it worth repeating: "God doesn't send anyone to hell; anyone who ends up there put themselves there by their own free will" (author unknown). Each of us has a choice. God wants so much for us to choose eternity with Him. If He were to force us, we would be no different than robots to Him. It must be our choice.

When we *all* stand before God in judgment—and we *all* will—God will say one of two things to us, as is stated in the Bible, either *"Well done, good and faithful servant"* (Matthew 25:23 NIV), or *"Then I will tell them plainly, 'I never knew you. Away from me, you evildoers!'"* (Matthew 7:23 NIV).

I know without a shadow of a doubt which statement I want to hear. And I know the response I am going to hear. I was once in a meeting with a military veteran who had PTSD; the guy who was with me, another Christ-follower, asked the man, "Do you know whether you will go to heaven or hell when you die?" The veteran said he was not sure. My friend's response was, "Well, let's make sure you will know the answer. Let's make sure you know the way to heaven." Peace comes from knowing the answer to this question!

I often say that the Bible is filled with warnings. God warns us about these things because He loves us! Many of these warnings are descriptions of what an eternity in hell looks like.

Picture the worst place on earth. Think of the worst scenario you can imagine. Hell is that—but with the absence of *anything* good. That is unimaginable to any of us still living on this earth. No police, no law and order to rescue you. *No one at all* will *ever* try to help you. There will never again be any love, any hope, or any light, just never-ending thirst, clawing and biting, (the gnashing of teeth), never-ending torment, perpetual heat, kicking, beatings, and who knows what else. It is the absence of God, the absence of *everything* good!

Please take these warnings seriously.

Biblical Descriptions of Hell

(taken from the Got Questions website)

It is a place of *"weeping and gnashing of teeth"* **(Matthew 25:30 NIV).**

We are cast out into hell on our own accord. We make the choice to go there. We choose the path to hell, where there is never-ending sorrow. Can you imagine—nonstop weeping, wailing, and sadness? There is also the gnashing of teeth. I looked up the definition of what this means; this is what it said: "anger, rage, hatred, grief, contempt, or derision (ridicule, mockery, contemptuous treatment)."

Therefore, the "gnashing of teeth" is a biblical expression that denotes anger, rage, hatred, grief, contempt, or ridicule. It is used in the Old Testament to describe the emotions of the wicked, the enemies and the deriders of God's people. It is also used in the New Testament to depict the torment and anguish of those who reject Christ and are excluded from the Kingdom of God. "Gnashing of teeth" conveys a vivid image of the severity of the pain unbelievers will experience.

Sadly, those who reject God will realize in hell what they have truly lost, and the realization that there will be no "second chance" will cause them to feel the full weight of the pain that goes with that knowledge. The anguish of being separated from God will never go away. It is eternal and unrelenting. And yet we all deserve that kind of punishment: *"For all have sinned and fall short of the glory of God"* (Romans 3:23 NIV), but God, in His mercy, has made it possible for us to avoid that eternal pain and suffering. Paul explains, *"For the wages of sin is death, but the gift of God is eternal life in Christ Jesus our Lord"* (Romans 6:23 NIV).

It is a place of *"outer darkness"* (Matthew 22:13 NKJV).

Jesus used the term *outer darkness* in the parable of the wedding feast to describe a condition of great sorrow, loss, and woe. It stands in vivid contrast to the brightly lit and joyous celebration attended by those who accept the King's invitation. Interpreting the wedding feast as heaven, the "outer darkness" must therefore be the place of eternal punishment. Most Bible scholars agree that the phrase *outer darkness* refers to hell or, more properly, the lake of fire (Matthew 8:12; 13:42; 13:50; and 25:30, 41).

The "outer darkness" of Jesus' parable is called the "blackest darkness" in Jude 1:13 (NIV). Again, a place of judgment is the obvious meaning, because it is reserved for "godless people" (verse 4 CEB). Perhaps the place of judgment is pictured as "dark" because of the absence of God's cheering presence, as described in this verse: "When you hide your face, they are terrified" (Psalm 104:29 NIV). God is called "light" in 1 John 1:5, and if He withdraws His blessing, only darkness is left. Throughout the Scriptures, light symbolizes God's purity, holiness, and glory. Darkness is used as a symbol of moral depravity (Psalm 82:5; Proverbs 2:13; Romans 3:12). Darkness can also refer to trouble and affliction (Job 5:12; Proverbs 20:20; Isaiah 9:2), and to death and nothingness (1 Samuel 2:9; Ecclesiastes 11:8; Job 3:4–6).

We also see a description of torment, sorrow, and everlasting destruction in these next three verses. Take the time to look them up for yourself. Something amazing happens when we open the Bible and open our hearts to the Word: a place of torments (Luke 16:23); a place of sorrows (2 Samuel 22:5–7); and a place of everlasting destruction (2 Thessalonians 1:9).

Below are several other verses I highly suggest you consider in your research. There is nothing more important than the warnings we have been given about our eternal destiny. Increasingly, many churches don't want to address these warnings. I'm not sure if it's due to a fear of causing a decline in attendance at their church or if they just don't have the courage to speak the truth as found in the Bible. Either way, this is why we as believers must take the time to read the Word ourselves and share them with those who are willing to listen. Here are the additional verses for your study—hell is:

- A place where people are tormented with fire and brimstone (Revelation 21:8 NKJV).
- A place of worms that don't die (Mark 9:44 NKJV).
- A place where the fire is not quenched (Mark 9:43 NKJV).
- A place where there is no rest (Revelation 14:11 NKJV).

- A place that will ultimately be a lake of fire (Revelation 20:14 NKJV).
- A place of hopelessness and unsatisfied desires (Luke 16:24 NIV).
- A furnace of fire (Matthew 13:42, 50 NKJV).
- A place of separation (Matthew 13:49 NKJV).
- A place filled with the cowardly, the unbelieving, the vile, the murderers, the sexually immoral, those who practice magic arts, the idolaters, and all liars (Revelation 21:8 NIV).
- A place shut out from the presence of the Lord and the majesty of His power (2 Thessalonians 1:9 NIV).
- A place where the fallen angels dwell (2 Peter 2:4; Jude 1:16 NIV).

*There is a saying I started to use early on in my walk with God: "The devil had a hold of me for so long, he's not going to let go that easy." The devil is very patient. It may seem like he and his army have fled from me, but I am aware they are very patient. They will wait for just the right opportunity to attack; even if it is in very small ways, it will be enough to get me off track. The enemy knows it could be the beginning of separating me from my walk and commitment with God. The devil is great at what he does, and he has had plenty of time to perfect his craft.

These are sobering warnings, please take them seriously!

Now that we have addressed the bad news, let's look at the Good News—no, the *Great* News! We know how the war ends—God wins! The prince of darkness will be defeated by the Prince of Peace.

All who accept the gift God has provided through the death and resurrection of Jesus Christ will escape the destiny of everlasting weeping and gnashing of teeth. Paul proclaims, *"If you declare with your mouth, 'Jesus is Lord,' and believe in your heart that God raised him from the dead, you will be saved. For it is with your heart that you believe and are justified, and it is with your mouth that you profess your faith and are saved"* (Romans 10:9–10 NIV). Jesus uses powerful imagery like "wailing" and "gnashing of teeth" to illustrate the importance of turning away from the sin that leads to hell and turning to Him, who alone provides salvation in heaven.

Biblical Descriptions of Heaven

(taken from the Got Questions website)

Jesus came to proclaim the Good News of the Kingdom of heaven. In Luke 4:43 (NIV), Jesus said, *"I must proclaim the good news of the kingdom of God to the other towns also, because that is why I was sent."*

Heaven is a real place described in the Bible. The word *heaven* is found 276 times in the New Testament alone. The Scriptures refer to three heavens. The apostle Paul was "caught up to the third heaven," but he was prohibited from revealing what he experienced there (2 Corinthians 12:1–9 NIV). If a third heaven exists, then there must also be two other heavens. The first is most frequently referred to in the Old Testament as the "sky" or the "firmament." This is the heaven that contains clouds, the area through which the birds fly. The second heaven is interstellar/outer space, which is the abode of the stars, planets, and other celestial objects (Genesis 1:14–18).

The third heaven, the location of which is not revealed, is the dwelling place of God. Jesus promised to prepare a place for true Christians in this heaven (John 14:2). Heaven is also the destination of the Old Testament saints who died trusting God's promise of a Redeemer (Ephesians 4:8). Whoever believes in Christ shall never perish, but shall have eternal life (John 3:16).

The apostle John was privileged to see and report on the heavenly city (Revelation 21:10–27). John witnessed that heaven (the new earth) possesses the "glory of God" (Revelation 21:11), the very presence of God. Because heaven has no night and the Lord Himself is the light, the sun and moon are no longer needed (Revelation 22:5).

The city is filled with the brilliance of costly stones and crystal-clear jasper. Heaven has twelve gates (Revelation 21:12) and twelve foundations (Revelation 21:14). The paradise of the Garden of Eden is restored: the river of the water of life flows freely, and the Tree of Life is available once again, yielding fruit monthly with leaves for the "healing of the nations" (Revelation 22:1–2 NIV). However eloquent John was in his description of heaven, the reality of heaven is beyond the ability of finite man to describe (1 Corinthians 2:9).

Heaven is a place of "no mores." There will be *no more* tears, *no more* pain, and *no more* sorrow (Revelation 21:4). There will be *no more* separation, because death will be conquered (Revelation 20:6). The best thing about heaven is the presence of our Lord and Savior (1 John 3:2). We will be face-to-face forever with the Lamb of God, who loved us and sacrificed Himself so that we can enjoy His presence in heaven for eternity.

Keeping all that in mind, heaven is:

- The place where the throne of God is situated (Deuteronomy 26:15; Psalm 11:4; Isaiah 66:1).
- A place where God will reward His people (Matthew 5:12).
- A place safe from theft and destruction (Matthew 6:20).
- A place of rejoicing (Luke 15:7).
- A place where there will be no marrying or giving in marriage (Matthew 22:29–30).
- A house with many rooms (John 14:2).
- A home of righteousness (2 Peter 3:13).
- A garden paradise (Revelation 2:7).
- A place that doesn't experience hunger, thirst, tears, or scorching heat (Revelation 7:16–17).
- A place of victory and the playing of harps (Revelation 15:2).
- A holy city (Revelation 21:2).
- A place where God will dwell with us (Revelation 21:3).
- A place that doesn't experience sadness, death, or pain (Revelation 21:4).
- A place of brilliance like that of very precious jewels. The walls are made of jasper, and the city is made of pure gold, as pure as glass. The foundations of the city walls are decorated with precious stones. The twelve gates are each made from one single pearl (Revelation 21:11, 18–21).
- A place that is lit by the glory of God (Revelation 21:23).

- A place with no night (Revelation 21:25).
- A place where no impure thing or person exists (Revelation 21:27).
- A place of life and healing (Revelation 22:1–3).
- A place where God and His people will reign forever (Revelation 22:5).

I know I said this in a previous chapter, but it is worth repeating. Knowing what the future holds for you personally is crucial. The devil wants nothing more for you not to believe any of this. But Jesus could only have been a liar, an insane person, or telling us the truth. For thousands of years, people have been trying to disprove His words, His miracles, and His resurrection, only to come up short. Many times, those people who search for the truth about Him end up converting from a non-believer to a believer.

Your choice is either to seek the wisdom that God offers or to rely on your own understanding. The results will determine where you spend eternity: in heaven or in hell.

The Key to Real Wisdom
(taken from the Bible App)

Would you ever build a house without blueprints? Or assemble an airplane without instructions? Or conduct open-heart surgery without first receiving training? Hopefully your answer is no! If we want to know how something works, we should look to the experts for insight. In a similar way, if we want to know how the world works, we should look to God, the One who created it.

> *The fear of the LORD is the beginning of wisdom, and the knowledge of the Holy One is insight.*
>
> —Proverbs 9:10 ESV

God made the world and everything in it. He knows how life works best. But too often, we look to ourselves or even to others to tell us who we are and what to think, and to explain to us how life works. The good news is that:

- Wisdom doesn't begin with us—the created.
- Wisdom begins with God—the Creator.

Are you interested in real wisdom? Genuine insight? True understanding? Look to God, study His ways, and consider His character. Examine Him closely and discover what you've been searching for.

Real wisdom starts with a God-centered foundation. Everything else must be built on that rock. But as we do that, we must first honestly ask ourselves some hard questions: *Do I want to learn from God, or would I rather do my own thing? Do I want godly wisdom, or would I rather be my own god?*

Satan fell from heaven because he wanted to have more power than God. Adam and Eve struggled in the Garden because they weren't sure whether they could trust God. And ever since, every human has been faced with the choice: to seek God or to seek life without Him. No one can make the decision for you, but if you want to be truly wise, you must choose God.

So, right now, be real with yourself: Are you willing to surrender your way of thinking and genuinely look to God, or would you rather just continue doing your own thing? If you feel a welling of pride rising up within you, ask God to help you knock it down. Brick by brick, He can reestablish your foundation.

5
Promises and Warnings

I'M GOING TO BE VERY forward in this chapter. Many people think of the Bible as a book filled with gentle and passive sayings. Until I started reading it myself, then diving into deeper study, I thought the same thing. But as I dug in, I started realizing there are many warnings in the Bible written for our benefit. I have often wondered why we have not heard as much about the warnings found in the Word of God. How can we be prepared when the enemy attacks if we don't understand who the enemy is or his tactics?

I know now that many churches do not like to preach the "hard things." Don't get me wrong, I love the promises that are found throughout the Scriptures from beginning to end, but I'm also a person who wants to know the truth, no matter how hard it is to hear.

In my men's Bible study group and other Christian groups in which I have been involved, I am known for saying this next phrase:

"The Bible is a book of promises *and warnings.*" I sometimes think that it makes many people uncomfortable when I point out the warnings found in Scripture. Good! We *should* be uncomfortable. Maybe we will take the warnings more seriously!

To me, the Bible is a love story. It is God's attempt to make sure we live the life that will lead us to spend eternity with Him, our Creator. But if we don't know *both* the promises and the warnings in His Word, how do you think we will be prepared for the battles we are going to experience? We won't be. We will be left unprepared, caught off-guard, and taken by surprise when trouble comes our way.

God loves us so much. He wants to make sure we are equipped for all situations. Studying the Bible, being in the Word every day, and through our relationship with the Father, with Jesus, and with the Holy Spirit does just that. Now, make sure the full armor of God is in place for you and memorize the verses below; they will prepare you!

Jesus said many tough things. He stood up to the Pharisees, and He was not afraid of the Romans. Our society today makes Jesus look like a pacifist; He was anything but. He came to earth and was fearless; He took on the devil and won; He went to the roughest areas and confronted sin! When you start learning His words, you will see that because of His love for us, He took on extremely difficult situations without fear.

I will start with a verse that has both a warning first, then is followed up with an amazing promise:

A Warning and a Promise

For the wages of sin is death, but the gift of God is eternal life in Christ Jesus our Lord.

—Romans 6:23 NIV

This verse has become a "life verse" for me. It is a verse I rely on in good times and in hard times. It is very direct and easy to understand, and it doesn't mince words.

A Promise

This is one of the most-recognized verses in the Bible. You will read a story later in chapter 8 of this book about Tim Tebow and this verse, John 3:16, that made millions of people Google its words.

For God so loved the world that he gave his one and only Son, that whoever believes in him shall not perish but have eternal life.

—John 3:16 NIV

A Very Dire Warning

"Not everyone who says to Me, 'Lord, Lord,' shall enter the kingdom of heaven. . . . Many will say to Me in that day, 'Lord, Lord, have we not prophesied in Your name, cast out demons in Your name, and done many wonders in Your name?' And then I will declare to them, 'I never knew you; depart from Me, you who practice lawlessness.'"

—Matthew 7:21–22 NKJV

I don't know about you, but this is something I do not want to hear when I am standing in front of our Lord! I can't say I didn't know any better. God will know those who decided to operate on their own understanding and ignore His message.

A Warning

If anyone turns a deaf ear to my instruction, even their prayers are detestable.

—Proverbs 28:9 NIV

Just wow! No additional words are needed.

A Promise

"I have told you these things, so that in me you may have peace. In this world you will have trouble. But take heart! I have overcome the world."

—John 16:33 NIV

A Warning

Jesus answered, "I am the way and the truth and the life. No one comes to the Father except through me."

—John 14:6 NIV

A Promise

I can do all this through him who gives me strength.

—Philippians 4:13 NIV

Please also read verses 11 and 12 prior to this verse.

A Warning

For where you have envy and selfish ambition, there you find disorder and every evil practice.

—James 3:16 NIV

A Promise

Grace and peace be yours in abundance through the knowledge of God and of Jesus our Lord.

—2 Peter 1:2 NIV

A Warning

"I am the vine; you are the branches. If you remain in me and I in you, you will bear much fruit; apart from me you can do nothing. If you do not remain in me, you are like a branch that is thrown away and withers; such branches are picked up, thrown into the fire and burned."

—John 15:5–6 NIV

A Promise

"If my people, who are called by my name, will humble themselves and pray and seek my face and turn from their wicked ways, then I will hear from heaven, and I will forgive their sin and will heal their land."

—2 Chronicles 7:14 NIV

A Warning and a Promise

"I tell you, whoever publicly acknowledges me before others, the Son of Man will also acknowledge before the angels of God. But whoever disowns me before others will be disowned before the angels of God. And everyone who speaks a word against the Son of Man will be forgiven, but anyone who blasphemes against the Holy Spirit will not be forgiven."

—Luke 12:8–10 NIV

I have included this entire chapter, as you read further.

A Warning

"Do not be afraid of those who kill the body but cannot kill the soul. Rather, be afraid of the One who can destroy both soul and body in hell."

—Matthew 10:28 NIV

A Promise

"Whoever acknowledges me before others, I will also acknowledge before my Father in heaven."

—Matthew 10:32 NIV

A Warning

"There is a judge for the one who rejects me and does not accept my words; the very words I have spoken will condemn them at the last day."

—John 12:48 NIV

A Promise

"But seek first his kingdom and his righteousness, and all these things will be given to you as well."

—Matthew 6:33 NIV

A Warning

A faithful person will be richly blessed, but one eager to get rich will not go unpunished.

—Proverbs 28:20 NIV

A Promise

For the Spirit God gave us does not make us timid, but gives us power, love and self-discipline.

—2 Timothy 1:7 NIV

A Warning

"What good will it be for someone to gain the whole world, yet forfeit their soul? Or what can anyone give in exchange for their soul?"

—Matthew 16:26 NIV

A Promise

Take delight in the LORD, and he will give you the desires of your heart.

—Psalm 37:4 NIV

A Warning

"Nothing impure will ever enter it, nor will anyone who does what is shameful or deceitful, but only those whose names are written in the Lamb's book of life."

—Revelation 21:27 NIV

Warnings and Encouragements

I have decided to include here the entire twelfth chapter of Luke. I believe this is such a powerful chapter in the Bible, it needed to be written out. In it, Jesus tells us what we need to do to avoid experiencing the dire warnings about future events, as well as the descriptions of hell, found in the book of Revelation. He was spelling out *eternity* in this chapter. He was demonstrating His love for us, for He does not want any of us to experience the seven years of tribulation, and certainly not an eternity separated from Him. In this chapter, specifically the section, Not Peace but Division (verses 49–53), has had a profound impact on my own walk and my surrender to God.

> *Meanwhile, when a crowd of many thousands had gathered, so that they were trampling on one another, Jesus began to speak first to his disciples, saying: "Be on your guard against the yeast of the Pharisees, which is hypocrisy. There is nothing concealed that will not be disclosed, or hidden that will not be made known. What you have said in the dark will be heard in the daylight, and what you have whispered in the ear in the inner rooms will be proclaimed from the roofs.*
>
> *"I tell you, my friends, do not be afraid of those who kill the body and after that can do no more. But I will show you whom you should fear: Fear him who, after your body has been killed, has*

authority to throw you into hell. Yes, I tell you, fear him. Are not five sparrows sold for two pennies? Yet not one of them is forgotten by God. Indeed, the very hairs of your head are all numbered. Don't be afraid; you are worth more than many sparrows.

"I tell you, whoever publicly acknowledges me before others, the Son of Man will also acknowledge before the angels of God. But whoever disowns me before others will be disowned before the angels of God. And everyone who speaks a word against the Son of Man will be forgiven, but anyone who blasphemes against the Holy Spirit will not be forgiven.

"When you are brought before synagogues, rulers and authorities, do not worry about how you will defend yourselves or what you will say, for the Holy Spirit will teach you at that time what you should say."

The Parable of the Rich Fool

Someone in the crowd said to him, "Teacher, tell my brother to divide the inheritance with me."

Jesus replied, "Man, who appointed me a judge or an arbiter between you?" Then he said to them, "Watch out! Be on your guard against all kinds of greed; life does not consist in an abundance of possessions."

And he told them this parable: "The ground of a certain rich man yielded an abundant harvest. He thought to himself, 'What shall I do? I have no place to store my crops.'

"Then he said, 'This is what I'll do. I will tear down my barns and build bigger ones, and there I will store my surplus grain. And I'll say to myself, "You have plenty of grain laid up for many years. Take life easy; eat, drink and be merry."'

"But God said to him, 'You fool! This very night your life will be demanded from you. Then who will get what you have prepared for yourself?'

"This is how it will be with whoever stores up things for themselves but is not rich toward God."

Do Not Worry

Then Jesus said to his disciples: "Therefore I tell you, do not worry about your life, what you will eat; or about your body, what you will wear. For life is more than food, and the body more than clothes. Consider the ravens: They do not sow or reap, they have no storeroom or barn; yet God feeds them. And how much more valuable you are than birds! Who of you by worrying can add a single hour to your life? Since you cannot do this very little thing, why do you worry about the rest?

"Consider how the wildflowers grow. They do not labor or spin. Yet I tell you, not even Solomon in all his splendor was dressed like one of these. If that is how God clothes the grass of the field, which is here today, and tomorrow is thrown into the fire, how much more will he clothe you—you of little faith! And do not set your heart on what you will eat or drink; do not worry about it. For the pagan world runs after all such things, and your Father knows that you need them. But seek his kingdom, and these things will be given to you as well.

"Do not be afraid, little flock, for your Father has been pleased to give you the kingdom. Sell your possessions and give to the poor. Provide purses for yourselves that will not wear out, a treasure in heaven that will never fail, where no thief comes near and no moth destroys. For where your treasure is, there your heart will be also.

Watchfulness

"Be dressed ready for service and keep your lamps burning, like servants waiting for their master to return from a wedding banquet, so that when he comes and knocks they can immediately open the door for him. It will be good for those servants whose master finds them watching when he comes. Truly I tell you, he will dress himself to serve, will have them recline at the table and will come and wait on them. It will be good for those servants whose master finds them ready, even if he comes in the middle of the night or toward daybreak. But understand this: If the owner of the house had known at what hour the thief was coming, he would not have let his house be broken into. You also must be ready, because the Son of Man will come at an hour when you do not expect him."

Peter asked, "Lord, are you telling this parable to us, or to everyone?"

The Lord answered, "Who then is the faithful and wise manager, whom the master puts in charge of his servants to give them their food allowance at the proper time? It will be good for that servant whom the master finds doing so when he returns. Truly I tell you, he will put him in charge of all his possessions. But suppose the servant says to himself, 'My master is taking a long time in coming,' and he then begins to beat the other servants, both men and women, and to eat and drink and get drunk. The master of that servant will come on a day when he does not expect him and at an hour he is not aware of. He will cut him to pieces and assign him a place with the unbelievers.

"The servant who knows the master's will and does not get ready or does not do what the master wants will be beaten with many blows. But the one who does not know and does things deserving punishment will be beaten with few blows. From everyone who has

been given much, much will be demanded; and from the one who has been entrusted with much, much more will be asked.

Not Peace but Division

[This section has had a profound impact on my life.]

"I have come to bring fire on the earth, and how I wish it were already kindled! But I have a baptism to undergo, and what constraint I am under until it is completed! Do you think I came to bring peace on earth? No, I tell you, but division. From now on there will be five in one family divided against each other, three against two and two against three. They will be divided, father against son and son against father, mother against daughter and daughter against mother, mother-in-law against daughter-in-law and daughter-in-law against mother-in-law."

Interpreting the Times

He said to the crowd: "When you see a cloud rising in the west, immediately you say, 'It's going to rain,' and it does. And when the south wind blows, you say, 'It's going to be hot,' and it is. Hypocrites! You know how to interpret the appearance of the earth and the sky. How is it that you don't know how to interpret this present time?

"Why don't you judge for yourselves what is right? As you are going with your adversary to the magistrate, try hard to be reconciled on the way, or your adversary may drag you off to the judge, and the judge turn you over to the officer, and the officer throw you into prison. I tell you, you will not get out until you have paid the last penny."

—Luke 12 NIV

A Promise

"I have told you these things, so that in me you may have peace. In this world you will have trouble. But take heart! I have overcome the world."

—John 16:33 NIV

I want to share more insights about this verse, and that is why I have repeated it here. John 16:33 has changed the way I walk through life. In it, Jesus let us know that even when we surrender to Him, we will still have trials and pain while on this earth. I understand now that those trials are for my benefit. This is a hard lesson for many people to grasp and a hard lesson to live through.

If we are true believers, when we suffer, our faith grows. If we were to just fall away at every tough situation, how strong would our faith have been to begin with? If we also had no suffering, would we ever reach out to God? God loves us so much; He wants us to reach out to Him like little children. When our little children have problems, or they get hurt, or they are afraid, they reach out to us, their parents, and we give them comfort.

All our troubles here on earth are temporary; they will disappear when we go from death to life—life with God. We all have a terminal illness, and none of us can escape it. We will all die. What is most important is what happens next, after death. Free will determines that answer. None of us will be able to blame God if we end up in hell. It will be by our own choice. Only we decide if we will spend eternity with God and Jesus or if we will send ourselves into the fiery furnace, where there is weeping, wailing, and gnashing of teeth. We either live by the flesh, or we live by the Spirit; we either see the bigger picture, or we live in this temporary existence. It's our choice.

There are so many more promises and warnings in the Bible, and I encourage you to read them for yourself. It is the only way you can truly have the understanding that is needed to navigate through this life.

I want to finish this chapter with Jesus' final words to us in the Bible, found in the book of Revelation. Please take the time to learn and study this Instruction Manual of Life for yourself. It will be your greatest investment.

> "Look, I am coming soon! My reward is with me, and I will give to each person according to what they have done. I am the Alpha and the Omega, the First and the Last, the Beginning and the End. Blessed are those who wash their robes, that they may have the right to the tree of life and may go through the gates into the city. Outside are the dogs, those who practice magic arts, the sexually immoral, the murderers, the idolaters and everyone who loves and practices falsehood. I, Jesus have sent my angels to give you this testimony for the churches. I am the Root and the Offspring of David, and the bright Morning Star."
>
> —Revelation 22:12–16 NIV

6

REPENT OR PERISH

LET'S START THIS CHAPTER BY clearing up the falsehood that the devil has recently tried to install in the younger generation and in many others. The enemy has tried to convince people that everyone will get into heaven, whether they repent or not. Let me ask you the question: Do you *really* think God will just welcome *unrepentant sinners* into heaven with open arms? A recent advertisement on television said this about God: "He gets us." While it is true that He understands us and empathizes without situation, this ad has convinced some people who are sinners that they will get a pass just because "He gets us." This is a lie, another tactic of the devil.

Let me make it as clear as I can: God does not accept everyone! Due to His holy nature, He cannot accept sin! He does not accept those who think they can live life according to their own ways, the ways of the world. Yes, God is a loving God, and He certainly loves all of us, but He is also a just God. God has made it abundantly clear to those who pay attention to his words that it is our choice: repent or perish!

So many people who have bought into the lie that everyone goes to heaven are going to be in for a rude awakening. The Bible is so very clear: we must repent of our sins, turn away from them, and ask for God's forgiveness.

I am sorry that some of us have heavier crosses to bear in this regard than others, but that is just the way it is. Again, everything we deal with on this earth is temporary! But being an unrepentant sinner comes with consequences that last for eternity. Don't be upset with me; I'm simply telling you what the Bible says. You can choose to believe that the Bible is the inspired Word of God and is from God, or you can follow your own understanding, or those trying to manipulate you into following the wide path that leads to destruction.

Paul traveled the known world at the time, spreading the Word, as commanded by Jesus, to as many people as he could. This is just one verse from the book of Acts that stood out to me concerning his ministry:

> "I have declared to both Jews and Greeks that they must turn to God in repentance and have faith in our Lord Jesus."
>
> —Acts 20:21 NIV

I will include several other verses about the topic we are discussing, but one thing is certain: you must repent. The theme of repentance is found throughout the Bible, and it has been the central message of the Church for thousands of years. It doesn't matter whether you like it or you disagree with it; it is what is written, and it is the core message Jesus came to share with us.

I absolutely love this quote from a book Jack Hibbs wrote titled *Living in the Daze of Deception*. (I cannot recommend this book enough.) Hibbs wrote: *"We can never appreciate Jesus Christ as Savior unless we first recognize that we need saving."*

So many people believe they are not in jeopardy of punishment, of God's wrath. As Ray Comfort has declared in his street preaching in California: We have broken God's moral law (The Ten Commandments); we will be found guilty on the Day of Judgment and sentenced. Ray points out, though, that there is a way out of this punishment. God provides a way for our penalty to be paid. We can't do it by our works, our deeds, or by trying to be good. Try that in a court of law: "Judge, I am sorry I committed that heinous crime, but I am a good person most of the time. Will you set me free?" No, you would be sentenced and put in prison.

The only way to be set free from the consequences of our sin is as Jesus told us in John 14:7 (NIV): *"I am the way and the truth and the life. No one comes to the Father except through me."* It is only through the death of Jesus that our penalty could be paid in full. If we repent (turn away from) our sins, be born again in the Spirit, and accept Jesus Christ as our Lord and Savior, then we will be saved.

Jack Hibbs went on to point out that when Jesus spoke to His followers, He announced, *"The kingdom of God has come near. Repent and believe the good news"* (Mark 1:15 NIV). He made things very clear! Hibbs went on to point out that pursuing Christ without changing course is impossible. It locks us into an endless cycle of sin and then seeking forgiveness, only to repeat the process again and again. True repentance breaks that cycle.

Unfortunately, many churches do not teach repentance. It seems they care more about filling seats in their auditoriums. They do not want to turn anyone away by telling them the hard truth—but it is the truth that will save their lives. This is very sad. Don't be one who misleads others, keeping them from receiving the gift of salvation simply because it's the hard thing to say. We are all here to help others find their way to eternity with God.

Let's take a look at what the Bible says about repentance. This makes me think of some great advice I heard Pastor Jack Hibbs once give. When you are asked a question that has to do with a stance you take that may be controversial, simply begin your answer with: "Well, the Bible says . . ." This makes your answer not just your opinion, but it is rooted in the Word of God, which we follow.

In Luke 13, the first eight verses are titled with the heading "Repent or Perish":

> *Now there were some present at that time who told Jesus about the Galileans whose blood Pilate had mixed with their sacrifices. Jesus answered, "Do you think that these Galileans were worse sinners than all the other Galileans because they suffered this way? I tell you, no! But unless you repent, you too will all perish. Or those eighteen who died when the tower in Siloam fell on them—do you think they were more guilty than all the others living in Jerusalem? I tell you, no! But unless you repent, you too will all perish."*
>
> —Luke 13:1–5 NIV

Peter replied, "Repent and be baptized, every one of you, in the name of Jesus Christ for the forgiveness of your sins. And you will receive the gift of the Holy Spirit."

—Acts 2:38 NIV

The Lord is not slow about His promise, as some count slowness, but is patient toward you, not wishing for any to perish but for all to come to repentance.

—2 Peter 3:9 NASB1995

Peter, an apostle of Jesus, didn't say we would all be accepted, or that we should just come as we are, or that we could create our own way. Second Peter 3:9 plainly states that we *will perish* without repentance. It is important not to lead people into believing that they can go on sinning and still make it to heaven.

He who conceals his transgressions will not prosper, but he who confesses and forsakes them will find compassion.

—Proverbs 28:13 NASB1995

When God saw their deeds, that they turned from their wicked way, then God relented concerning the calamity which He had declared He would bring upon them. And He did not do it.

—Jonah 3:10 NASB1995

From that time Jesus began to preach and say, "Repent, for the kingdom of heaven is at hand."

—Matthew 4:17 NASB1995

"Therefore remember from where you have fallen, and repent and do the deeds you did at first; or else I am coming to you and will remove your lampstand out of its place—unless you repent."

—Revelation 2:5 NASB1995

And Jesus answered and said to them, "It is not those who are well who need a physician, but those who are sick. I have not come to call the righteous but sinners to repentance."

—Luke 5:31–32 NASB1995

But because of your stubbornness and unrepentant heart you are storing up wrath for yourself in the day of wrath and revelation of the righteous judgment of God.

—Romans 2:5 NASB1995

Men were scorched with fierce heat; and they blasphemed the name of God who has the power over these plagues, and they did not repent so as to give Him glory. Then the fifth angel poured out his bowl on the throne of the beast, and his kingdom became darkened; and they gnawed their tongues because of pain, and they blasphemed the God of heaven because of their pains and their sores; and they did not repent of their deeds.

—Revelation 16:9–11 NASB1995

These verses are just a handful of passages from the Bible that make it abundantly clear that God and Jesus want us to know the importance of our repentance. The world will try to deceive you into believing you can go on living the way you are living. The idea that when we die, we all go to heaven, and we all end up in a good place is misleading—entirely false. The Scriptures say different. Jesus had a direct and much different message.

I must go back to the tactics of the devil. He wants to keep you from knowing the truth, keep you from reading the Bible, and keep you from having the knowledge that Jesus came to give us. This is Satan's way of hurting God—by taking you away from Him. The battle we face is for our very souls. Do not rely on your own understanding or what society would try to have you believe. The penalty is too great not to research this for yourself. Start a daily routine of studying God's Word. Commit to learning it and growing your relationship with God, our Father, through His Son, Jesus Christ. This is the best way to combat the devil's tactics.

What Does It Mean "to Perish"?

The next verse we will consider was an eye-opener for me. I realized God's angels will actually separate me because of the choices I make with my free will. If we choose not to learn and obey God's Word, we will only have ourselves to blame when the angels come to separate us from Him.

> *"Once again, the kingdom of heaven is like a net that was let down into the lake and caught all kinds of fish. When it was full, the fisherman pulled it up on the shore. Then they sat down and collected the good fish in baskets, but threw the bad away. This is how it will be at the end of the age. The angels will come and separate the wicked from the righteous and throw them into the blazing furnace, where there will be weeping and gnashing of teeth.*

"Have you understood all these things?" Jesus asked.

—Matthew 13:47–51 NIV

This is just one parable in which Jesus spoke to His disciples in terms they would understand in their day. We have the luxury of a Bible that has been written out for us. For thousands of years, mankind has studied it and passed it on, and yet so many still choose to ignore what Jesus came to warn us about.

I personally love the parables Jesus spoke. They stick in our memories in the same way a story or a good book does. Jesus' next parable is also sobering; again, because of free will, we get to choose to listen and abide with God, or to ignore Him, but then pay the penalty when the time comes. And it *will* come. We tend to live for this moment in time, not realizing or preparing for eternity and what comes next.

The Parable of the Weeds

Jesus told them another parable: "The kingdom of heaven is like a man who sowed good seed in his field. But while everyone was sleeping, his enemy came and sowed weeds among the wheat, and went away. When the wheat sprouted and formed heads, then the weeds also appeared.

"The owner's servants came to him and said, 'Sir, didn't you sow good seed in your field? Where then did the weeds come from?'

"'An enemy did this,' he replied.

"The servants asked him, 'Do you want us to go and pull them up?'

"'No,' he answered, 'because while you are pulling the weeds, you may uproot the wheat with them. Let both grow together until the harvest. At that time I will tell the harvesters: First collect the weeds

and tie them in bundles to be burned; then gather the wheat and bring it into my barn.'"

—Matthew 13:24–30 NIV

The disciples had difficulty understanding this parable, so Jesus explained it in plain terms:

"The one who sowed the good seed is the Son of Man. The field is the world, and the good seed stands for the people of the kingdom. The weeds are the people of the evil one, and the enemy who sows them is the devil. The harvest is the end of the age, and the harvesters are the angels.

"As the weeds are pulled up and burned in the fire, so it will be at the end of the age. The Son of Man will send out his angels, and they will weed out of his kingdom everything that causes sin and all who do evil. They will throw them into the blazing furnace, where there will be weeping and gnashing of teeth. Then the righteous will shine like the sun in the kingdom of their Father. Whoever has ears, let them hear."

—Matthew 13:37–43 NIV

You may think this is harsh. You may even ask, "How can a loving God do this?" But God has given us every chance to accept Him and His words. God loves us so much. He has done everything so that we would have access to His Word. He has been patient so that it can spread around the world, and yet so many people still reject it and Him. He came to earth incarnated to show us the way, and again so many rejected Him. They lived by their own understanding instead of surrendering to Him.

Remember, the next time He comes, it will be like a thief in the night; there will be no time to prepare. We must stay prepared for when that day comes. The best way to do that is to begin a daily routine. Invest your time and treasure in Him. Commit yourself to developing a relationship with Him. If you can't spend twenty minutes each morning with God and Jesus, why would you expect Him to work in your life? At the end of this book, I will share details on how to start preparing and how to stay in His Word until that day comes. We must keep the full armor of God on and ready to go every day if we expect to stay on that narrow, less-traveled path.

> *"Enter through the narrow gate. For wide is the gate and broad is the road that leads to destruction, and many enter through it. But small is the gate and narrow the road that leads to life, and only a few find it."*
>
> —Matthew 7:13–14 NIV

7

THE UNLIKELY DISCIPLES

Tribute to Matt Sr. and Karey Shaw

WHAT IS MY PURPOSE? DO I have a biblical one? Me? Why in the world would God use me?

I didn't truly give myself to Christ until I was in my mid-fifties. Now, as I am writing this book, I am about to turn sixty years old. I could have never imagined the amazing transformation that I was about to embark upon. I have always believed in God, and that Jesus was His Son, but that was about the extent of how much I acknowledged God.

God is so good. All I can say is, "Thank You, God, for waiting for me!" He never gives up on us. We are the ones who give up or never take the time to look up to find Him. He is always right there. God is waiting for us to stop long enough in our self-made, self-absorbed, busy lives here on this earth to take that first and oh-so-important step. It is a leap of faith!

I love the simplicity of what God asks of us: *"Draw near to me and I will draw near to you."* The action requested in this verse is simple, but of the utmost importance. We must take the first step! Because God gave us free will, this is the only possible way.

As simple as this verse begins, however, the beautiful result is that once we take the first step, God then draws near to us. He loves us so much that He does not want to lose us—not even one of the one hundred, even if the other ninety-nine are following Him! (I will explain this later in the book.)

Now, I realize I am quickly passing through my time here on earth. Our time on this earth is extremely brief. What I do in this very short length of time will have rewards or consequences regarding what is next to come for me in eternity—yes, eternity! I love the words of Psalm 78:39 (NIV). In this psalm, David recalls God's grace in relation to the people He has made: *"He remembered that they were but flesh, a passing breeze that does not return."* (I suggest searching right now on YouTube for Francis Chan's original rope illustration. It is a quick four-minute and twenty-second video about time that provides a great perspective of our time on this earth.)

It really doesn't matter at what age we surrender ourselves to the Lord. All that matters is that we do it. I wish I'd had the knowledge, the desire, and the guidance to surrender earlier in life. It just wasn't in the cards I was dealt. Many people have been dealt worse hands, however, and I am grateful I was able to find my way to Him before my time here is over. My hope and purpose for writing this book is that you also will truly surrender yourself before your short and brief time on this earth is done. What is next to come will last much longer!

I love this quote: "If you are not willing to live for Christ now, what makes you think you will be willing to die for Him later?" If you understand the book of Revelation, you will understand what this quote is saying. If you don't, I would suggest studying the book of Revelation, because it is a very important question to which you should have an answer.

Many people have heard about the great "lifting up." Those of us who have accepted Jesus as our Lord and Savior, and have surrendered ourselves to Him, will be lifted up before the Great Tribulation period. This is because we live for Christ *now*. But what is to come after that moment, in the blink of an eye, will be almost unimaginable. Do you think at that time you will be able to withstand the antichrist and be willing to die for Jesus then?

Unlikely Beginning

Jesus could have chosen anyone when He began His ministry. The likely choice, if He wanted power and influence, would have been to gather the Pharisees and the great Sanhedrin under His influence. His disciples would have looked more like the people of religious stature, such as Caiaphas and Nicodemus. If He wanted power, He would have used the Romans and the full force of the Roman empire to rule over the people. He is God! He could have used anyone and could have been born anywhere and at any time.

But God chose the humblest of beginnings when He sent His "one and only Son" to the earth. He picked the most unassuming village, Nazareth, a place that many in the region knew very little about, and the ones who did, looked down upon the village as if it was not worthy of much. Most followers have heard the phrase, "Can anything good come out of Nazareth?" Ironically, the only thing on this earth that is truly good came out of this small, unassuming, humble village.

Most of us, if given the choice of where we would want to be born and raised, in those times, would have picked a palace. We would have picked a place where everything was given to us, where everything was provided and easy. But our God picked a barn in a tiny village with no privileges offered to Him. Our God entered this world in the humblest of ways! He was laid in an animal's feed trough. We make it sound better by calling it a "manger," but it was a feed trough in a barn, where animals literally ate.

Jesus came to this earth in the humblest way, and He left in the most brutal way! He did this because He loves us so much. At the end of time, all He wants is for all His children (His sheep) to return to Him, the same as any father would want!

Moving forward, I will be pointing out some people around us in our current day who are "unlikely disciples." I will follow that by "unlikely disciples from the Old Testament" whom God chose, along with those whom Jesus chose in the New Testament. This is meant to help us all gain a better understanding of what it means to be a disciple. You may ask: Are there certain qualifications? Could a sinner like me be a disciple? If we study who has been picked by God throughout time for some amazing missions, I think we will see that we are *all* qualified for what God has already asked of us.

I hope you enjoy the rest of this chapter. I pray it helps you fulfill the purpose God has for you!

The Great Commission

This is found in the last chapter of the gospel of Matthew. as Jesus commissioned His followers to go forth and make disciples.

> *Then Jesus came to them and said, "All authority in heaven and on earth has been given to me. Therefore go and make disciples of all nations, baptizing them in the name of the Father and of the Son and of the Holy Spirit, and teaching them to obey everything I have commanded you. And surely I am with you always, to the very end of the age."*
>
> —Matthew 28:18–20 NIV

Definition of a *Disciple of Christ*:

A disciple of Christ is someone who is following Jesus, is being changed by Jesus, and is committed to the mission of Jesus (see disicipleship.org).

Unlikely Disciples: Matt Sr. and Karey Shaw

A very close friend of mine and brother in Christ, Matt Shaw, introduced me to his dad, Matt Sr. Matt and I have helped each other through the journey of finding a closer relationship with Christ. I suggest that everyone find that person on whom you can lean in both good times and rough times, because both will come.

When I first met Matt Shaw Sr., I was so inspired by his sacrifice and dedication to helping others. Shortly after, I met his wife, Karey. Right away, I was able to see God working through both of them.

Matt Sr. and Karey were ready to retire. They had earned it! Matt had grown up in California; then he served in Vietnam and worked hard his entire life. Matt Sr. is part of our men's group at church, Iron Sharpens Iron. One day he told us his story, and it truly inspired me to do more to share God's Word and lead people to Christ. His story began when he recognized a need for someone to help the homeless not far from the area where they lived. He prayed that the homeless in this area would be able to get the help they needed. He was not expecting God to answer with: *What about you?* I love how he answered the subtle question: "Me?" I don't think that was the answer to his prayer that he was hoping for. He likely expected there to be someone else who would be able to help those in need.

God bless Matt Sr and his wife, Karey! They were obedient to what God put in their hearts, even though that meant their retirement would drastically change from what they had envisioned it to be. For the past several years, Matt and Karey have been providing hot food, coffee, Bibles, and more to the homeless in their area. They eventually started a little mission called "The Streets of the Lost and Found" in Riviera Beach, Florida.

Matt Sr. and Karey are such an inspiration—not only to me, but to so many others. I love the fact that neither of them had any formal Bible training, but still God chose them to spread His message and love. They have lived their lives with many of their own hardships and challenges, but they knew that when God called them, they needed to listen and answer that call.

Another Unlikely Disciple: Billy Graham

Billy Graham was known around the world for spreading the Gospel, but he truly came from humble beginnings, having been raised on a dairy farm in North Carolina. When Billy was sixteen years old, a Christian businessman secured a deal to hold an all-day prayer meeting on the Grahams' family farm. Billy knew then that he wanted to pursue the Lord.

One day he went back into the woods, laid his Bible down on a stump, and prayed that God would show him that it was the inspired Word of God—every word of it. Billy left those woods with a pure and true faith. He went from humble beginnings to creating what has become a globally recognized ministry. His story speaks of God's faithfulness in response to simple obedience. Billy Graham himself brought countless numbers of people to the Lord, giving them the chance to choose salvation through his crusades, and inspiring so many with his remarkable, unshaken faith that endured through some of the toughest decades, wars, and political upheavals. To this day, his ministry continues on even now that he has gone on to heaven.

An Unlikely Disciple, Jack Hibbs

Jack Hibbs was an abortion survivor. He now leads one of the biggest churches in the country.

On Christmas Eve, 1957, Hibbs says his mother "put her two older children to bed in their apartment, boiled a metal clothes hanger and proceeded to lie down on the kitchen floor, where she attempted to abort her third child." Hibbs told *Calvary Chapel Magazine* that "fortunately, someone came to his mother's rescue and the abortion failed." She went to the hospital, and twenty-one days later, on January 15, 1958, "God saw fit to let me come into a world where I wasn't wanted."

God had different plans for Jack. Pastor Hibbs now pastors one of the largest churches, Calvary Chapel, in Chino Hills, California. He is known for taking on some of the toughest topics in today's world and preaching the Bible boldly.

Simon Peter, an Unlikely Disciple and Apostle of Christ (New Testament)

Simon Peter is the next person on whom I would like to focus. Most people in Simon's day would likely have never imagined him being chosen to walk with Jesus, the Messiah. But Jesus chose a roughneck fisherman from a tiny village in an unimpressive part of the world to build His Church upon. To this day, millions, if not billions, of people know his name and his story.

Simon Peter was one of the first followers of Jesus Christ. He was an outspoken and ardent disciple, one of Jesus' closest friends, an apostle, and a "pillar" of the Church. Peter was enthusiastic, strong-willed, impulsive, and at times, brash. For all his strengths, Peter failed several times in his life. Still, the Lord who chose him continued to mold him into exactly who He intended Peter to be.

Simon was originally from Bethsaida, and he lived in Capernaum; both were cities on the coast of the Sea of Galilee. He was married, and he and James and John were partners in a profitable fishing business. Simon met Jesus through his brother, Andrew, who had begun to follow Jesus after hearing John the Baptist proclaim that Jesus was the Lamb of God. Andrew immediately went to find his brother to bring him to Jesus as well. Upon meeting Simon, Jesus gave him a new name: *Cephas* (in Aramaic) or *Peter* (in Greek), which means "rock." Later, Jesus officially called Peter to follow Him, producing a miraculous catch of fish. Immediately, Peter left everything behind to follow the Lord.

For the next three years, Peter lived as a disciple of the Lord Jesus. Being a natural-born leader, Peter became the *de facto* spokesman for the Twelve. More significantly, it was Peter who first confessed Jesus as "the Christ, the Son of the living God," a truth Jesus said was divinely revealed to Peter.

Peter was part of the inner circle of Jesus' disciples, along with James and John. Only those three were present when Jesus raised the daughter of Jairus and when Jesus was transfigured on a mountain. Peter and John were also given the special task of preparing the final Passover meal. In several instances, Peter showed himself to be impetuous to the point of rashness. For example, it was Peter who left the boat to walk on the water toward Jesus—then promptly took his eyes off Jesus and began to sink. It was also Peter who took Jesus aside to rebuke Him for speaking of His death, and he was swiftly corrected by the Lord. It was Peter who suggested erecting three tabernacles to honor Moses, Elijah, and Jesus, but he then fell to the ground in fearful silence at God's glory. It was Peter who drew his sword and attacked the servant of the high priest at Jesus' arrest and was immediately told to sheath his weapon. It was Peter who boasted that he would never forsake the Lord, even if everyone else did, but he later denied three times that he even knew the Lord.

Through all of Peter's ups and downs, however, Jesus remained his loving Lord and faithful Guide. Jesus reaffirmed Simon as Peter, the "Rock," and promised that he would be instrumental in establishing Jesus' Church. After His resurrection, Jesus specifically named Peter as one who needed to hear the Good News. And, repeating the miracle of the large catch of fish, Jesus made a special point of forgiving and restoring Peter, recommissioning him as an apostle.

On the Day of Pentecost, Peter was the main speaker to the crowds in Jerusalem, and the Church began that day with an influx of about three thousand new believers. Later, Peter healed a lame beggar and preached boldly before the Sanhedrin. Even arrest, beatings, and threats could not dampen Peter's resolve to preach the Good News of the risen Christ.

Jesus' promise that Peter would be foundational in building the Church was fulfilled in three stages: First, Peter preached on the Day of Pentecost. Then, he was present when the Samaritans received the Holy Spirit. Finally, he was summoned to the home of the Roman centurion Cornelius, who also believed and received the Holy Spirit. In this way, Peter "unlocked" three different worlds and opened the door of the Church to Jews, Samaritans, and Gentiles.

Even as an apostle, Peter experienced some growing pains. At first, he resisted taking the Gospel to Cornelius, a Gentile. However, when he saw the Romans receive the Holy Spirit in the same manner that he had, Peter concluded, "God does not show favoritism." After that, Peter strongly defended the Gentiles' position as believers and was adamant that they did not need to conform to Jewish law.

Another episode of growth in Peter's life concerns his visit to Antioch, where he enjoyed the fellowship of Gentile believers. However, when some legalistic Jews arrived in Antioch, Peter, to appease them, withdrew from the Gentile Christians. The apostle Paul saw this as hypocrisy and called it such to Peter's face.

Later in life, Peter spent time with John Mark, who wrote the gospel of Mark based on Peter's remembrances of his time with Jesus. Peter wrote two inspired epistles, 1 and 2 Peter, between AD 60 and 68. Jesus said that Peter would die a martyr's death' this prophecy was fulfilled, presumably, during Nero's reign. Tradition has it that Peter was crucified upside down in Rome, and although the story may be true, there is no scriptural or historical witness to the particulars of Peter's death (see Gotquestions.org).

Saul of Tarsus/Paul, an Unlikely Apostle of Christ (New Testament)

Saul/Paul was a persecutor, one who imprisoned and killed the Christians of his day. I don't think there could be a more unlikely disciple. Jesus could have chosen anyone to spread His message to the Gentiles (non-Jews). But Paul ended up spreading the message of the risen Christ, the Messiah, to not only the surrounding areas, but to Rome, which changed the course of history.

Again, God used Paul's time in prison to spread the Word to many other inmates, but also to the Roman soldiers. Below is another detailed account by *Gotquestions.org* about the life of Paul.

I believe the lives of Peter and Paul are very important, and I wanted to include the details of their lives before they encountered Jesus.

There is much we can learn from the life of the apostle Paul. Far from ordinary, Paul was given the opportunity to do extraordinary things for the Kingdom of God. The story of Paul is a story of redemption in Jesus Christ and a testimony to the fact that no one is beyond the saving grace of the Lord. However, to gain the full measure of the man, we must examine his dark side and what he symbolized before becoming "the apostle of grace." Paul's early life was marked by religious zeal, brutal violence, and relentless persecution of the early Church. Fortunately, the later years of Paul's life show a marked difference as he lived his life for Christ and the advancement of His Kingdom.

Paul was born as Saul, in Tarsus in Cilicia around AD 1–5. This was a province in the southeastern corner of modern-day Tarsus, Turkey. He was of Hebrew ancestry—with his lineage coming from the tribe of Benjamin. His parents were Pharisees—fervent Jewish nationalists who adhered strictly to the Law of Moses and sought to protect their children from "contamination" by the Gentiles. Anything Greek would have been despised in Saul's household, yet he could speak Greek and passable Latin. His familial household would have spoken Aramaic, the official language of Judea. Saul's parents were Roman citizens, but they viewed Jerusalem as a truly sacred and holy city.

At the age of thirteen, Saul was sent to Judea to learn from a prominent rabbi named Gamaliel, under whom Saul mastered Jewish history, the Psalms, and the works of the prophets. His education would continue for five or six years as Saul learned such things

THE UNLIKELY DISCIPLES

as dissecting Scripture. During this time, he developed a question-and-answer style of teaching known in ancient times as "diatribe." This method of articulation helped rabbis debate the finer points of Jewish law to either defend or prosecute those who broke the law. Saul went on to become a lawyer, and all signs pointed to his becoming a member of the Sanhedrin, the Jewish Supreme Court of seventy-one men who ruled over Jewish life and religion. Saul was zealous for his faith, and this faith did not allow for compromise. This zeal led Saul down the path of religious extremism.

In Acts 5:27–42, Peter delivered his defense of the Gospel and of Jesus in front of the Sanhedrin, which Saul would have been present to hear. Gamaliel was also in the session—he even delivered a message to calm the council after Peter's message and prevent them from stoning Peter. Saul might also have been present at the trial of Stephen—we know he was present for Stephen's stoning and death, for he held the garments of those who carried out the stoning. After Stephen's death, "a great persecution broke out against the church in Jerusalem," and Saul was a part of this. He became determined to eradicate all Christians, ruthless in this pursuit as he believed he was acting in the name of God. Arguably, there is no one more frightening or more vicious than a religious terrorist, especially when he believes he is doing the will of the Lord by killing innocent people. This is exactly what Saul of Tarsus was—a religious terrorist. He states, "He began ravaging the church, entering house after house, and dragging off men and women, he would put them in prison."

The pivotal passage in the story of Paul's transformation is found in Acts 9:1–22, which recounts Paul's meeting with Jesus Christ on the road from Jerusalem to Damascus, a journey of about

150 miles. Saul was angered by what he had seen and filled with murderous rage against the Christians. Before departing on his journey, he asked the high priest for letters to the synagogues in Damascus, requesting permission to find any Christians—followers of "the Way"—and bring them back to Jerusalem to imprison them. On the road to accomplish this task, Saul was caught in a bright light from heaven that caused him to fall face-down on the ground, then he heard the words, "Saul, Saul, why are you persecuting Me?" He replied, "Who are You, Lord?" Jesus answered directly and clearly, "I am Jesus, whom you are persecuting." This might not have been Saul's first encounter with Jesus, as some scholars suggest that young Saul might have known of Jesus and that he might have actually witnessed His death.

From that moment on, Saul's life was turned upside down. The light of the Lord blinded him, and as he traveled on, he had to rely on his companions. As instructed by Jesus, Saul continued to Damascus to make contact with a man named Ananias, who was hesitant at first to meet Saul because he knew Saul's reputation as an evil man. But the Lord told Ananias that Saul was a "chosen instrument" to carry His name before the Gentiles, before kings, and to the children of Israel, and he would suffer for doing so. Ananias followed the Lord's instructions and found Saul, on whom he laid hands, and told him of his vision of Jesus Christ. Through prayer, Saul received the Holy Spirit, regained his sight, and was baptized. Saul immediately went into the synagogues and proclaimed Jesus as the Son of God. The people were amazed and skeptical, as Saul's reputation was well known. The Jews thought he had come to take away the Christians, but he had, in fact, joined them. Saul's boldness increased as the Jews living in Damascus were confounded by Saul's arguments proving that Jesus was the Christ.

Saul spent time in Arabia, Damascus, Jerusalem, Syria, and his native Cilicia, and Barnabas enlisted his help to teach those in the church in Antioch. Interestingly, the Christians who had been driven out of Judea by the persecution that arose after Stephen's death are the ones who founded this multiracial church.

Saul took his first of three missionary journeys in the late AD 40s. As he spent more time in Gentile areas, Saul began to go by his Roman name, Paul. Paul wrote many of the New Testament books. Most theologians are in agreement that he wrote the books of Romans, 1 and 2 Corinthians, Galatians, Philippians, 1 and 2 Thessalonians, Philemon, Ephesians, Colossians, 1 and 2 Timothy, and Titus. These thirteen "letters" (epistles) make up the "Pauline Authorship" and are the primary source of his theology. As previously noted, the book of Acts gives us a historical look at Paul's life and times. The apostle Paul spent his life proclaiming the risen Christ Jesus throughout the Roman world, often at great personal peril. It is assumed that Paul died a martyr's death in the mid-to-late AD 60s in Rome.

So, what can we learn from the life of the apostle Paul? First, we learn that God can save anyone. The remarkable story of Paul repeats itself every day as sinful, broken people all over the world are transformed by God's saving grace in Jesus Christ. Some of these people have done despicable things to other human beings, while some just try to live a moral life thinking that God will smile upon them on the Day of Judgment. When we read the story of Paul, we are amazed that God would allow into heaven a religious extremist who had murdered innocent women and children. Today, we might see terrorists or other criminals as unworthy of redemption because their crimes against humanity are just too great. But the story of Paul is a story that can be told today—he isn't worthy in our eyes of a second chance, yet God granted him mercy. The truth is that every person matters to God, from the "good," "decent," average person to the "wicked," "evil," degenerate one. Only God can save a soul from hell.

Second, we learn from the life of Paul that anyone can be a humble, powerful witness for Jesus Christ. Arguably, no other human figure in the Bible demonstrated more humility while sharing the Gospel of Jesus Christ as Paul. Acts 20:19 tells us that he "[served] the Lord with all humility and with tears and with trials that happened to [him] through the plots of the Jews" (ESV). In Acts 28:31, Paul shares the Good News of Jesus Christ: "Boldly and without hindrance he preached the kingdom of God and taught about the Lord Jesus Christ." Paul was not afraid to tell others what the Lord had done for him. Paul spent all his days, from his conversion to his martyrdom, working tirelessly for the Kingdom of God.

Finally, we learn that anyone can surrender completely to God. Paul was fully committed to God. In Philippians 1:12–14, Paul wrote from prison, "I want you to know, brothers, that what has happened to me has really served to advance the gospel, so that it has become known throughout the whole imperial guard and to all the rest that my imprisonment is for Christ. And most of the brothers, having become confident in the Lord by my imprisonment, are much more bold to speak the word without fear." Despite his circumstances, Paul praised God and continually shared the Good News (see also

Acts 16:22–25 and Philippians 4:11–13). Throughout his hardships and suffering, Paul knew the outcome of a life well lived for Christ. He had surrendered his life fully, trusting God for everything. He wrote, "For to me to live is Christ, and to die is gain" (Philippians 1:21 ESV). Can we make the same claim?

I will finish up by listing others through whom God chose to spread His message. No matter your background, your education, or your doubts, if you reach out to God, He will work in your life. One thing to understand is that it will be in His time, and He knows what is good for you better than you do. His will be done, not ours. Don't be disappointed if all you ask for is not given. God knows what's best, and He doesn't make mistakes!

God uses unlikely people to lead His mission to continue Jesus' mission on the earth. (I am another example of proof of this!)

- Abraham: He was old and took a slave woman to have a baby at his wife's request.
- Elijah: He was suicidal.
- Joseph: He was abused.
- Moses: He had a speech problem, and then he killed a man.
- Gideon: He was filled with fear.
- Samson: He was a womanizer and disobedient to the Lord.
- Rahab: She was a prostitute.
- Samaritan woman at the well: She was divorced; she'd had five husbands.
- Noah: He was an alcoholic.

- Jeremiah: He was very young and wanted nothing to do with the visions God gave him.
- Jacob: He was a cheater who deceived his father.
- David: He sent a man to his death so he could take the man's wife.
- Jonah: He ran from God and refused to follow His instructions.
- Martha: She was full of anxiety and worried about everything.
- Zacchaeus: He was small of stature and money hungry.
- Mary Magdelene: She was a prostitute.
- Matthew: He was a tax collector, looked down upon by all the Jews.

It is obvious that God uses flawed people! Maybe it's because that is all He has to choose from.

8

Inspiring Thoughts, Writings, and Stories

OVER THE YEARS I HAVE been inspired to write down my thoughts, along with some dreams and other content that has come from what I have learned, studied, and observed. Again, these are my own thoughts; I am certainly not a scholar, nor do I pretend to have gained any kind of formal biblical education. I simply love the Lord and want to try to help others receive the gift I have been given.

#1: Why don't people follow Jesus?

There may be several reasons why people don't want to know more about Jesus and the time He spenton the earth. The time Jesus spent teaching, still to this day, has had the biggest impact on civilization than any other event or person in our history. I take this from some of my own experiences and thoughts. Once a person understands what is at stake, how can they just turn the other way? But they do!

I'm not trying to offend anyone, but I think this is an important question that needs honesty in its answer: Why do people not want to know more about Jesus and His teachings? Here are some answers I've come up with:

1. People are too lazy to invest the time to learn more.
2. People listen to the naysayers and don't bother educating themselves to make an educated decision for themselves.
3. People say, "Well, I'm a good person, and if God is a good God, I'll be alright." If people took the time to learn what the Bible says, they would know it takes more than that to get to heaven.
4. People are more concerned about what is happening in this world and in their own lives. They are not thinking about what will happen after their short time here on this earth. So many people are so consumed with things like their appearance, their possessions, what others think about them, their job status, or their social status in general.
5. People just don't believe. Maybe it is based on how they were raised, or they have other beliefs, or they have never been exposed to the teachings of Jesus.
6. People are embarrassed to admit their beliefs or to come out as Christians to their peers. They don't want to be that "religious fanatic" in the crowd.

7. People like their worldly lifestyle of partying, drinking, drugs, sexual encounters, and other immoral activities.

Many people are afraid to know more about Jesus! But if they put in the effort to learn, they might realize that everything Jesus was trying to get us to understand is true, and that would drastically change their lives. Once you understand what Jesus is saying to you, you have to make some very big changes. Your old way of living likely will need to fade away, or at the very least, be altered—unless you were, in a rare occurrence, already living a Christ-like life.

Here are just a few things Jesus taught:

1. Be selfless. Put others before yourself. Serve others as Jesus did.
2. Be humble. Put God first before all else.
3. Be generous. Give your best to God. He wants to see that your faith is strong and that you trust Him. This includes giving of your finances, as well as your time.
4. Surrender yourself to Him.
5. Confess your sins to God.
6. Repent of your sins.
7. Love your neighbor.
8. The only way to the Father is through the Son.

To do what Jesus taught takes commitment, faith, discipline, love, and more. I can say from experience, however, that it is worth every bit of effort it takes!

#2: Tim Tebow's 3:16 Story

You may have already heard this story, but in case you have not, it will bless you to read it here first. Even though I have heard this story many times, it never gets old. We do serve an amazing God!

Let us start with the most recognized verse itself:

> "For God so loved the world that he gave his one and only Son, that whoever believes in him shall not perish but have eternal life."
>
> —John 3:16 NIV

Tim Tebow's Shocking Story about John 3:16 "Coincidence" Goes Viral

A video of former NFL quarterback Tim Tebow recalls an amazing biblical "coincidence" in his life is going viral on social media.

The story begins when Tebow was in his college football years. In 2009 he was weeks away from competing in the National Championship game, which would be highly televised.

Tebow, in his video, said God led him to write *John 3:16* under his eyes for all the world to see while he played.

In the video, Tebow goes on to say, "The next six weeks leading up to the game I was really agonizing and contemplating what verse and God kept bringing up to my heart and my head John 3:16, which is the essence of our Christianity. It is the essence of our hope."

After winning the National Championship game, Tebow found out something incredible happened during the game: 94 million people Googled the verse John 3:16.

INSPIRING THOUGHTS, WRITINGS, AND STORIES

"Honestly my first thought was, 'How do 94 million people not know John 3:16?" He went on to say, "I was just so humbled by how big the God is that we serve."

But that's not where the story ends.

Looking ahead three years to 2012, Tebow is now a Denver Bronco QB, he's playing the Pittsburg Steelers in the playoffs, and after the Broncos won, he was headed into the post-game press conference, when his public relations representative stopped him in his tracks.

"He says, 'Timmy, did you realize what happened?' I was like, 'Yeah, we just beat the Steelers. We're going to play the Patriots.' And he was like, 'No, do you realize what happened?'" Tebow shared.

"He said, 'It's exactly three years later from the day that you wore John 3:16 under your eyes," Tebow continued. "I was like, 'Oh, that's really cool.'"

"He said, "No, I don't think you realize what happened. During the game you threw for 316 yards, your yards per completion were 31.6, your yards per rush were 3.16, the ratings for the night were 31.6, the time of possession was 31.06, and during the game 91 million people Googled John 3:16. It's the number-one trending thing on every platform,'" Tebow shared.

"I was just standing there in the hallway about to do this press conference just thinking that that night was about a football game. It really wasn't . . . we serve such a big God," he continued.

Tebow believes God did something miraculous that night.

"The God that we serve is a God of miracles," he said. "I just have to be willing to step out and say, 'Here You go, God. I'm going to give You my fish and my loaves of bread and watch what He does with it."

*Source: CBN The Christian Perspective

#3: Faith, Not Fear

The only thing you should truly fear is living a life separated from God and then dying in your sins. These are some of my goals in spreading His message:

- To help Christians live like Christians.
- To live in the Word and in faith.
- To be a light that leads non-believers to Christ, giving them hope for eternity.
- To not conform to fear, but to be led to contentment through Christ.
- To not conform to hate that divides God's people.

The woman who touched Jesus' robe took a great risk. She had been bleeding for many years, and the Pharisees would have deemed her unclean. By touching a rabbi, she risked being severely punished. It would have been commonly known in those days that touching Him would make Him unclean as well.

When "Jesus called out, 'Who touched me?' Peter replied, 'Many people are touching You'" (Luke 8:45 VOICE). Many other people might have been touching Jesus, but this woman's faith is what Jesus felt. After touching Him, she was healed. Jesus turned to her and said, just as He declared to many whom He had made

INSPIRING THOUGHTS, WRITINGS, AND STORIES

whole, "Your faith has healed you" (Luke 8:48 NIV). Here are some observations about this woman and the fear she had experienced:

- Her faith was stronger than her fear.
- For the past few years, fear has gripped the hearts of both believers and non-believers.
- How strong is a believer's faith if they are living in constant fear?

Scriptures concerning Fear

- "We may boldly say, The Lord is my helper, and I will not fear what man shall do unto me" (Hebrews 13:6 KJV).
- "Do not be anxious about anything, but in every situation, by prayer and petition, with thanksgiving, present your requests to God. And the peace of God, which transcends all understanding, will guard your hearts and your minds in Christ Jesus" (Philippians 4:6–7 NIV).
- "Fear not, for I am with you; be not dismayed, for I am your God. I will strengthen you, yes, I will help you, I will uphold you with My righteous right hand" (Isaiah 41:10 NKJV).
- "Peace I leave with you; my peace I give you. I do not give to you as the world gives. Do not let your hearts be troubled and do not be afraid" (John 14:27 NIV).

Scriptures concerning Faith

- "And whatever you ask in prayer, you will receive, if you have faith" (Matthew 21:22 ESV).

- "And without faith it is impossible to please him, for whoever would draw near to God must believe that he exists and that he rewards those who seek him" (Hebrews 11:6 ESV).

- Throughout the gospels, whenever Jesus healed someone, He would say, "Your faith has healed you," or "Your faith is beautiful."

#4: Worldly Distractions

Causing us to lose sight of the Lord because of worldly distractions is a tool of the devil. We are seeing this happen daily in our country. These distractions are designed to take our focus off God and the mission Jesus has given to us. The enemy essentially says, "Look over here while something else is going on over there."

As the time of Jesus' Second Coming draws near, the distractions will become more frequent. The devil knows he is running out of time. He is trying to destroy marriages, separate families, and pit brother against brother, sister against sister, and kids against their parents. He will use every tactic this world has to offer: greed, lust, envy, power, lies, division, social media, politics, even pandemics. You name it, he will try to use it.

Know the Bible—and I mean, know it *in your heart*, not just what the words say. The Bible says that even the devil knows the words found in Scripture. Unless you apply this Book to your everyday life, you will be subject to the destruction the devil attempts to cause (Ephesians 6:11). Put on the full armor of God!

More Distractions

- Gas prices, inflation, Critical Race Theory, the open border, abortion, the supply chain, the transgender agenda. While it is important to pay attention to political issues, too many believers are turning all their energy toward worldly issues ahead of seeking God first. God wants us to fulfill His mission, the one He sent His Son to tell us about. Save people, change hearts, turn to God, and pray in all situations.
- The closer you get to God, the farther you move away from sin.
- Don't waste your time trying to change minds—change hearts and let God do the rest.
- Start with God, not with social media!

The following bullet points are notes I took from my pastor's message in a service on July 4:

- Our nation was founded on God and godly principles. Don't let society tell you otherwise. We are "one nation under God."
- George Washington, Thomas Jefferson, Patrick Henry, Ben Franklin, and many other founders all invoked God! They didn't advocate for our country to exist apart from Him. Thomas Jefferson started the policy of prayer in schools, and George Washington is quoted as saying, "Learn all you can about the ways of Jesus."
- The idea of the separation of church and state being a part of the Constitution is a lie! It is actually from a letter written to

the Danbury Baptist Church from Thomas Jefferson, assuring them there would not be a state-run church that ruled over all other churches (like Russia or China has now).

- The state should not have an influence over the Church; the Church should have an influence over the state. Our founders understood that, absent of God, our nation would collapse under the weight of its sin—all the sins we now are seeing in our society.

- The Washington Monument (which is the center of our government) has God's name inscribed on it; the first inscription reads, "Holiness to the Lord"; the second reads, "In God we Trust"; and the third reads, "Search the scriptures. Hidden are the words *Laus Deo* = Praise be to God." Does this sound like the center of a government whose founders wanted to rid its land of God?

- In the 1960s, the Supreme Court removed prayer from schools. Our morals have been on a steady decline ever since.

- In the 1980s, they removed the Ten Commandments from schools and courthouses, claiming the separation of church and state. Again, this is a lie.

- We have kicked God out of our government, our schools, and our way of life, and now people are surprised by the consequences!

- How can we heal? God has showed us the way in 2 Chronicles 7:14 (NLT): *"Then if my people who are called by my name will humble themselves and pray and seek my face and turn from their wicked ways, I will hear from heaven*

INSPIRING THOUGHTS, WRITINGS, AND STORIES

and will forgive their sins and restore their land." We need revival—not distractions! This is God's promise, His plan.

- We must turn from our sins (repent). When times are good, we tend to drift away from God and think we don't need Him. But when trials come, we tend to run to Him. Draw near *always*; repent and pray—*always*!

- To repent, you first must know the Word. To obey God, you must know the Word. If you do not, then where will you get your direction? Don't let it be from the media, from Hollywood, from sports figures, from entertainers, or from any other worldly source! Sadly, this is what is happening in our world today.

#5: All In

Are you all in with God and Jesus?

- Have you truly surrendered? Or have you just surrendered what you are comfortable with surrendering? Are you all in?

- Are you too busy some days to worship, to thank, to pray, or to have a relationship with our God? How would you feel if God were too busy for you?

- When you have been in need, reached out for God, and found He was there for you, you were probably *all in* at that time. Will you only be *all in* when you are in need? The Scriptures are very specific when they say: *"Love the Lord your God with **all** your heart and with **all** your soul and with **all** your mind and with **all** your strength"* (Mark 12:30

NIV, emphasis mine). Also consider the words of Proverbs 28:9: *"If anyone turns a deaf ear to my instruction, even their prayers are detestable"* (NIV).

- If we are to expect all the glory and promises God has offered us, wouldn't you think He might expect us to give our all? We can't be check-the-box Christians and expect to please to God. He requires and deserves more than just part of us. He is asking for our *all*—be *all in*!

- If you are still holding on to things in your past, if you have not truly forgiven someone in your life and have not moved on from that offense, then you have not done what God has asked you to do.

- If you are living in fear, not trusting God fully, you are basically saying, "Well, God, I know You've got my back, but just in case, I'm going to do it my way anyway" (HGY6!!).

- If you are living with hatred for anyone, then you are falling into the devil's trap. Hatred is not from God, so that leaves us knowing where it comes from. We must forgive all, just as God has forgiven us.

- If you are living with anxiety, then you are not truly trusting God. If you are doing everything according to God's will and plan for you, then you should be able to overcome anxiety. In Philippians 4:13 (NIV), Paul states, *"I can do all things through Christ that strengthens me."* Before this amazing verse, Paul wrote these words: "*I am not saying this because I am in need, for I have learned to be content in any and every situation, whether well fed or hungry, whether living with plenty or in want"* (verses 11–12 NIV). Then, in verse 13, he wrote: *"I can do all things through Christ that strengthens me."*

- To be a true Christ-follower, it takes more than just saying, "I'm a Christian." It takes living according to God's specific instructions—and that means *all* of them! Here are some of the instructions I have found in the Bible:

  ◆ You must *be born again*: This also includes being baptized, which a public announcement of your faith to the world. All this must be done of your own free will.

  ◆ You must *pray*: Follow God's instructions to pray continuously, daily, always.

  ◆ You must *listen to Him and for Him*: take the time to listen; don't be "too busy."

  ◆ You must *believe in Him*, not just partially, but with all your heart, soul, mind, and strength.

  ◆ You must *obey Him*, not just in the areas where you want to obey, but in *all* areas.

  ◆ You must *love Him*, unconditionally, just as He loves us.

  ◆ You must *share Him*: Go and make disciples of men! God has sent us out on a mission, which is to continue the mission Jesus started. If we don't do this, then what Jesus sacrificed will have been for nothing.

  ◆ You must *serve Him*: In all we do, we must be as a servant, just as Christ was for us.

- You must *be willing to suffer*: Don't hide your faith when something might seem difficult or you find yourself in an awkward situation.

J.D. Greear has shared this great analogy: "When you look at a breakfast plate of eggs and bacon, you should think of the hen and the pig. They both had a part in providing that breakfast. The hen supplied the egg, but the pig was *all in*."

#6: Renegade

The true light which gives light to everyone, was coming into the world. He was in the world, and the world was made through him, yet the world did not know him. He came to his own, and his own people did not receive him. But to all who did receive him, who believed in his name, he gave the right to become children of God, who were born, not of blood nor of the will of the flesh nor of the will of man, but of God.

—John 1:9–13 ESV

Jesus' first coming to the earth was a lot like a great Western movie: at a desolate time, in a desolate place, the stage was set for an unlikely Hero to emerge; only instead of the gun-slinging cowboy riding in to save the town, the Hero was Jesus, and He was coming to save the world.

Yet the world did not know Him.

—John 1:10 ESV

INSPIRING THOUGHTS, WRITINGS, AND STORIES

Think of it! God, our Creator, walked among His creation for the purpose of saving us, and we had no clue. But why would we? First, He was too average-looking to be noticed: *"He had no form or majesty that we should look at him, and no beauty that we should desire him"* (Isaiah 53:2 ESV). Second, He was too poor to be impressive. According to the Law, a lamb was the required sacrifice for the atonement of sin, unless someone was too poor to afford one, in which case, two doves or pigeons could be offered instead: *"And when the time came for [Mary and Joseph's] purification according to the Law of Moses, they brought [Jesus] up to Jerusalem to present him to the Lord . . . and to offer a sacrifice according to what is said in the Law of the Lord, 'a pair of turtledoves, or two young pigeons'"* (Luke 2:22, 24 ESV). Third, He was from Nazareth, a town so small and off the beaten path that it was considered uneducated and backwoods, full of hicks and sticks: *"Philip found Nathanael and said to him, 'We have found him of whom Moses in the Law and also the prophets wrote, Jesus of Nazareth, the son of Joseph.' Nathanael said to him, 'Can anything good come out of Nazareth?'"* (John 1:45–46 ESV).

> *He came to His own, and His own did not receive Him.*
>
> —John 1:11 NKJV

Jesus was raised in Nazareth, but He did not stay there. When He claimed to be the Messiah, they rejected Him. Then they ran Him out of town on a rail, just like what happened to many heroes in the old Western movies: *"When [the people of Nazareth] heard these things, all in the synagogue were filled with wrath. And they rose up and drove [Jesus] out of town and brought him to the brow of the hill on which their town was built, so that they could throw him* down the cliff. But passing through their midst, he went away" (Luke 4:28–30 ESV).

> But to all who received him . . .
>
> —John 1:12 TLB

Besides faith, there were no requirements for having a relationship with Jesus—no status, no age, no race, no gender; no prior education or track record of good behavior. The greater the transgression, the greater the forgiveness. Jesus welcomed the poor, the rich, the meek, and the intelligent. He, in fact, broke every cultural, political, and social boundary in pursuit of us all: *"There is neither Jew nor Greek, there is neither slave nor free, there is no male and female, for you are all one in Christ Jesus"* (Galatians 3:28 ESV).

> He gave the right to become children of God.
>
> —John 1:12 TLB

Through Jesus, we lay claim to heaven's territory—its rights and its riches. Jesus became our Brother, our God, and our Father: *"But as it is, they desire a better country, that is, a heavenly one. Therefore God is not ashamed to be called their God, for he has prepared for them a city"* (Hebrews 11:16 ESV).

So yes, it was tough to recognize Jesus as the Messiah, the Hero, especially because He had no striking features. How He acted and those whom He chose to spend time with did not set Him apart either. But those who got it, those who followed the Renegade once their eyes were opened, reaped the reward. And so can we! With Him we become our own kind of renegade. With Jesus, we ride or die!

INSPIRING THOUGHTS, WRITINGS, AND STORIES

Questions to Ask

- What is most striking to you about the way Jesus began His ministry years?
- Jesus repeatedly extended His hand to all types of people. In what ways do you need to be more like Him? Whom do you struggle to welcome?
- In what ways are you a renegade for Jesus? In what ways do you need to become more of one?

#7: God's Wide Receivers

On December 15, 2021, I had a dream. In it, I saw myself, and all of us, in the world, as wide receivers for God, working on the end goal to get to eternity through this tough and fallen world.

In this scenario, God is the quarterback, who is always throwing us the pass. We must choose whether to make the effort to catch the ball, even though we might get hit. We might even have a penalty thrown on us, but we know we will advance the ball if we catch it. The defenders are the evil ones. If God throws that pass and we just do nothing with it, we must go back to the line of scrimmage, and we might even get an off-sides penalty and go backward.

The best part is that when God throws those passes, and we catch those passes, as we continue to fight hard for every yard, moving closer and closer to the end zone, we finally get that touchdown pass that brings us into eternity. It was hard work. We took some beatings along the way. We might have been disappointed with a bad pass, or there might have been a missed pass interference call, but we trusted in our heavenly quarterback. All the while, we had others around us helping us get to the goal line, and we tried to help our teammates achieve the same objective. Then, finally: touchdown! We have made it to eternity. It was all worth the effort! Don't stop fighting for every yard—the end goal is so worth the effort.

#8 Notable Quotables

The following are quotes I have heard and collected over the years. Some were overheard in sermons, others I found along the way in my journey (my apologies for not knowing all the authors' names), and some I actually came up with myself.

- "Everything to have a successful life is found in the Bible!"
- "Helping one person might not change the whole world, but it could change the world for that one person."
- "Death can be your finish line, or it can be your starting line to eternity."
- "If you want to talk to God, you first have to believe you can hear from Him."
- "It's better to humble yourself than to have God do it for you."
- "God uses ordinary people to do extraordinary things."
- "Do you worship the Creator or things He created?"
- "God uses broken people because that's all He has to work with."
- "No matter what my situation is, I will always have joy, because I know I have salvation. Knowing this, what

can possibly ruin my joy? It doesn't get any better than salvation!"

- "What unites us is greater than what divides us."
- "Integrity is when your walk matches your talk."
- "There are many ways to get to hell, but only one Way to get to heaven."
- "We don't need more knowledge; we need to be more obedient."
- "Seeking God needs to be our first priority, not our last resort."
- "There is no one so bad that they can't be saved, and there is no one so good that they don't need to be saved."
- "Eternity is too long to be wrong."
- "Our nation has become biblically illiterate."
- "I ask a lot of those who follow Me and very little of those who do not" (Jesus, in *The Chosen*).
- "Jesus came to separate those who want to follow Him from those who want to reject Him."
- "Religion is nothing without a relationship."
- "Are you living your life for eternal life or for this life? You can't do both!"
- "Sticks and stones may break your bones, but words can kill your soul."
- "Do you know what an ungodly person who has everything wants? Just a little more!"

- "There is a war raging for your soul. God wants it, and the devil wants it. Neither of them will force the outcome—that is all left up to you."

- "People, places, and things can never replace our eternal reward. None of those things even comes close to measuring up to what God has in store for us."

- "You cannot find true comfort in anything other than Christ. Everything else is just temporary."

- "All pain and suffering are just temporary. How we respond to it will determine whether our eternity will be with God or without God."

- "Just because we live in a godless culture doesn't mean we have to have a godless culture live in us."

- "You'll never know that God is all you need until God is all you've got."

- "Stay ready; then you won't have to get ready."

- "You will either spend eternity with God or without God. Free will gives you that choice. Just as the doors of the ark closed, so will the opportunity to be with God."

- "You won't be able to say no to the devil unless you've said yes to Christ."

- "The secret of endurance is to remember that your pain is temporary, but your reward will be eternal."

- "If you look at the world, you'll be distressed. If you look within, you'll be depressed. But if you look at Christ, you'll be at rest! Your focus will determine your feelings."

INSPIRING THOUGHTS, WRITINGS, AND STORIES

- "God's not interested in prisoners; we are all free to come or go."
- "A closed mouth doesn't get fed. Ask and you shall receive" (Zack Williams).
- "The world can't take away what the Lord has given us."
- "A little more like Jesus, a little less like me."
- "Don't just fight like a man. Fight like a man of God."
- "Sin provides you with temporary pleasure, but eventually it causes you nothing but pain."
- "God opens doors that no man can shut and shuts doors that no man can open" (Jack Hibbs).
- "We need to be more afraid of the judgment of God than the government, society, friends, or family" (Jack Hibbs).
- "The warnings in the Bible are not meant to scare us; they are meant to prepare us."

#9: What Will God Judge Us On?

It won't be our business success.

It won't be our works or our deeds.

It won't be our social media likes.

It won't be how busy we were.

It won't be how much wealth we stored up.

It won't be how much money we made.

It won't be the degrees we have achieved.

He will judge us on the amount of time we spent with Him.

He will judge us on how much we meditated on His Word.

He will judge us on how much we spread His message of salvation to others.

He will judge us on our obedience to Him and His Word.

He will judge us on whether we abided in Him and His Word.

He will judge us on how we treated other people, His children.

He will judge us on whether we put Him first or the world. Seek the Kingdom of God first!

He will judge us on whether we praised Him as the one and only God.

Most of all, He will judge us on whether we have accepted His Son as our Lord and Savior, who died on the cross as a sacrifice for our sins so that we can spend eternity with Him.

9

THE RAPTURE AND THE TRIBULATION

IF YOU MADE IT TO this chapter, you have already read some hard things. So many people do not realize the warnings that Jesus gave in the New Testament. There were also many warnings throughout the Old Testament, which most Christians know even less about.

Don't get me wrong, there are also so many amazing promises and beautiful things to look forward to, as you read about in previous chapters, but we must understand the whole picture. The problem is, many people do not understand that the path can be brutal if they don't abide in God's Word while they have the chance to do so. It has already been spelled out for us; the rest is up to us. The Rapture of the Church will be a beautiful experience for those of us who have followed God's words, repented of our sins, accepted Jesus as our Lord and Savior, and truly believe all this in our hearts. You can't fake it; God knows!

What comes next after God's people are caught up in the air to be with Him—in other words, raptured? Jesus has promised to come back like a "thief in the night," in the "twinkling of an eye" to collect His Church. Afterward, true Christians will be gone from this earth. What is next for those who remain will be nothing short of hell on earth. This is known as the Tribulation.

This information isn't meant to scare you, but it is frightening, and it should alarm you if you do not know Jesus. My hope for everyone who reads this book is that you will be caught up with me and brought home to our final destination to be united with our true Father.

The Bible says that once we are saved, we are "ambassadors of Christ". I love this! We now represent God's Kingdom. We are not citizens of this world any longer. We are citizens of heaven.

I once heard the following explained this way, and it stuck with me: If I was hired as an ambassador of the United States, I would be a representative of the United States. If the country I was an ambassador to was Italy, I would be the American ambassador to Italy. But if I fell in love with Italy more than I loved my own country, I wouldn't be a very good ambassador, now, would I?

This is what happens once we are ambassadors of heaven. If we love the world more than we love God, we will jeopardize our citizenship in heaven. It's a choice we get to make, but there are consequences or rewards attached to that choice. Now let's dig into what the Bible says about these two events, the Rapture and the Tribulation, which have been prophesied to take place. All other prophecies to date have taken place with complete accuracy. These two were promised and are still to come. At this point, nothing else

THE RAPTURE AND THE TRIBULATION

has to happen for the Rapture to take place. Everything that needs to be fulfilled has already taken place.

The Rapture (being caught up in the air)

> *The Coming of the Kingdom of God*
>
> *Once, on being asked by the Pharisees when the kingdom of God would come, Jesus replied, "The coming of the kingdom of God is not something that can be observed, nor will people say, 'Here it is,' or 'There it is,' because the kingdom of God is in your midst." Then he said to his disciples, "The time is coming when you will long to see one of the days of the Son of Man, but you will not see it. People will tell you, 'There he is!' or 'Here he is!' Do not go running off after them. For the Son of Man in his day will be like the lightning, which flashes and lights up the sky from one end to the other. But first he must suffer many things and be rejected by this generation. Just as it was in the days of Noah, so also will it be in the days of the Son of Man. People were eating, drinking, marrying and giving in marriage up to the day Noah entered the ark. Then the flood came and destroyed them all. It was the same in the days of Lot. People were eating and drinking, buying and selling, planting and building. But the day Lot left Sodom, fire and sulfur rained down from heaven and destroyed them all. It will be just like this on the day the Son of Man is revealed. On that day no one who is on the housetop, with possessions inside, should go down to get them. Likewise, no one in the field should go back for anything. Remember Lot's wife! Whoever tries to keep their life will lose it, and whoever loses their life will preserve it. I tell you, on that night two people will be in one bed: one will be taken and the other left. Two women will be grinding grain together; one will be taken and the other left."*
>
> —Luke 17:20–35 NIV

When Jesus says one woman would be left, He was saying that they would be left behind to face the seven years of the Tribulation. Some movies have tried to depict this future time on earth. The *Left Behind* series captured this in theory, but not to the magnitude of the true-life event that is to come. The other movie that portrayed this event is *The Remaining*. In my opinion, I think this movie captures this event the best it could be captured.

Still, a movie cannot come close to capturing the fear, anxiety, and despair of what it will feel like in that moment to be left behind, especially for those who have some knowledge of the Rapture but didn't believe it would actually happen.

I had a dream one night not long ago in which I thought this event happened and I had been left behind. I believe God showed me that night what true fear was—it was the worst nightmare I have ever experienced. It felt so real, like I was actually living what was happening. The end of the dream showed me it was not the Rapture that took place. Even still, this dream will always be in my memory. I truly hope everyone reading this book does the research for themselves concerning what the words of the Bible say about this prophetic event. The following passages address this event:

- 1 Thessalonians 4:16–18
- 1 Corinthians 15:51–53 (Paul saw the third heaven, see 2 Corinthians 12:2)
- John 14:1–3
- Matthew 24:36–41

- 2 Thessalonians 2 (I suggest reading this entire chapter; it may not address the Rapture, but it contains a dire warning and instructions for what to do when this event comes)

Below is a letter Tina and I wrote to the kids; we sent one to Deanna and a separate one to Michael. We love them so much, and we wanted to make sure they understood what has been prophesied about what is to come.

Deanna/Michael,

I wanted to write this letter because if what we believe that was written thousands of years ago does happen, Tina and I want you and Deanna/Michael to understand what the Bible wrote about this event.

The Bible is a book with many prophecies from the Old Testament and in the New Testament. Many of these prophecies have come true with such accuracy that once I started to study them it reinforced my faith.

As you both know, I didn't grow up with a strong belief in the Bible. I did, however, always believe in God, but I had very little understanding. I did also believe in Jesus, but I had even less understanding in His teachings.

Once I realized, in my fifties, that Jesus had been raised from the dead (the evidence is powerful), I knew that if God had come to earth, I needed to study what was written about His time here. I had never been taught what was written, so, in turn, I never provided that teaching to either of you. I do wish I had. You are both adults now, and this is now your personal choice, just as it was mine.

This letter is not to try to convince you of anything. It is solely to explain a prophecy that may or may not be fulfilled in my lifetime. If it doesn't happen, then no harm is done. But if it does, I wanted you both to understand what was written about it. The governments will not provide the answers.

So, the Bible speaks of an event that it terms the Rapture. This actual term, however, is not found in the Bible. The phrase used in the Bible is "being caught up." In brief, the Bible says that Jesus will return in the twinkling of an eye. He will take up His Church (His followers who believe, abide, surrender, and are born again), and afterward, a great Tribulation will begin that will last for seven years. This is described as hell on earth, mainly in the book of Revelation. There will be an Antichrist who will be in a battle for people's souls. This will be the ultimate battle between good and evil.

Now, the purpose of this letter may sound crazy, but if, all of a sudden, thousands of people are missing, including me and Tina, I want you both to know what was written about this event. The government will come up with all types of explanations—my guess would be aliens, ha ha—but some people will know of these prophesied teachings.

I would rather you both think I'm crazy or some kind of a religious nut, than not to know if this does happen in our lifetimes. Below are some verses that talk about this event; I have also included a list of some movies that have depicted it the best they could.

I love you both so much, and if I truly have conviction in my faith and didn't share this with you, I would be a horrible father.

What is the Rapture? The word **rapture** *comes from the Latin translation of the phrase "caught up."*

First Thessalonians 4:17 says, "Then we who are alive, who are left, will be suddenly caught up together with them in the clouds to meet the Lord in the air. And so we will always be with the Lord." Other verses include 1 Corinthians 15:51–53; John 14:1–3; Matthew 25:31–32; 1 Thessalonians 4:13–18; and Matthew 24:36–41. There are many other writings on this topic. The movie ***The Remaining*** *explains what life will be like after the Rapture. And the movie* **A Case for Christ** *gives a true story that is what made me initially research Jesus' teachings on this topic.*

Someone once said this to me, and it stuck: Jesus was either crazy, He was a liar, or He actually was who He said He was. He couldn't be just a "good man," because that would have made Him a liar. If He was crazy, then how do we explain all the miracles and the evidence of the resurrection? He couldn't be a prophet, either—prophets can't lie. He claimed to be the Son of God. If God came to the earth, I realized I needed to know everything I could learn about it!

Love, Dad and Tina!

The Tribulation (What Comes after the Rapture)

Here is a brief definition of this upcoming period of time:

The *Tribulation period* is a future time of God's judgment and discipline for the world and for Israel. It will last for *seven years* and be divided into two or three eras. According to Scripture, the Church will be raptured (caught up with Christ in the air) before the Tribulation period begins. The Antichrist will then rise to power and persecute Israel and the believers. The Tribulation will end with the battle of Armageddon and the return of Jesus Christ.

Detailed Explanation

I wanted to share a great observation that I heard: "If you're not willing to live for Jesus now, what makes you think you will be willing to die for Him later?" (Pastor Jack Hibbs).

The book of Revelation paints a very ominous picture of what is to come in the seven years of the Tribulation. This time has also been spoken of throughout both the Old and New Testaments. God wanted to give us these warnings. He does not want any of us to experience this wrath or perish. That is why He provides a way to avoid this time that is to come.

Regarding the above quote from Pastor Hibbs, if we are living for Christ now, we won't be left behind to face these seven years of tribulation. If you are left behind to experience this terrifying time that is to come, the only way to receive eternal life with God will be to stand with Jesus throughout extreme persecution and the horrific times up to your death. The rest of this chapter will explore some of the terrible things that have been written about this period, along with the warnings of its coming.

What Is the End-Time Tribulation?

The *Tribulation* is a future seven-year period when God will finish His discipline of Israel and finalize His judgment of the unbelieving world. The Church, comprised of all who have trusted in the Person and work of the Lord Jesus, will not be present during the Tribulation.

God sent Jesus as His last and final warning. The Bible is full of such joy and wonderful promises that God wanted us to know about. But He also wanted to tell us how to obtain all His amazing promises. God has made it abundantly clear that we must choose Him. He also has made the consequences abundantly clear for all who have ears to hear and for all who have eyes to see.

THE RAPTURE AND THE TRIBULATION

The following is provided by Bible.org:

(1) Revelation 4:1–2: John, a symbol of the Church, is taken up to heaven.

(2) Daniel 9:27: The Antichrist signs a covenant for seven years with the nation of Israel. This is the event that inaugurates the Tribulation period.

(3) Revelation 6:1–2: Christ opens the first of the seven sealed scrolls, and the rider on the white horse (probably the Antichrist) appears, using diplomacy and the promise of peace to establish his one-world government.

(4) Revelation 6:3–4: The second seal introduces a great world war.

(5) Revelation 6:5–6: The third seal begins the suffering of famine and inflation (the aftermath of war).

(6) Revelation 6:7–8: The fourth seal results, as do all wars, in death, but in this case it totals one-fourth of the people and living creatures on the earth. By today's population standards, that would amount to one and a half billion people.

(7) Revelation 6:9–11: This passage introduces the martyrdom of those who are converted under the preaching of the 144,000 Jewish witnesses described in chapter 7. An innumerable number of people receive Christ and are martyred by the government leader and harlot (the religious system described in chapter 17), who gets her power from the Antichrist. Note that evangelism during this period is back in the hands of the Jews. Since the Church is absent, the 144,000 apostle Paul–type believers will make powerful evangelists.

(8) Revelation 6:12–17: This sixth seal exhibits the wrath of God poured out in the form of a mighty earthquake, the likes of which has never been experienced before. It is so severe that people call on the rocks to fall on them.

(9) Revelation 8:1–6: The seventh seal introduces the seven trumpet judgments, ending the first quarter of the Tribulation period and preparing for an even worse period, called the "day of His [God's] wrath."

(10) Revelation 8:7: The first trumpet judgment results in one third of all trees and green grass being burned up by hail, fire, and blood cast upon the earth.

(11) Revelation 8:8–9: The second trumpet sees a great mountain of sulfur falling into the sea and destroying a third of the sea and all living creatures in it, and a third of the shipping vessels. Think of *The Poseidon Adventure* multiplied times one third of all the world's ships!

(12) Revelation 8:10–11: The third trumpet causes a great star (or meteor) called *Wormwood* (or "bitter") to fall on the fountains of water and a third of rivers to turn bitter, resulting in the deaths of millions.

(13) Revelation 8:12: The fourth trumpet results in one-third less sun, moonlight, and stars, extending the darkness of the night.

(14) Revelation 8:13: A special eagle flies around the earth, warning that worse judgments are to come.

(15) Revelation 9:1–12: The fifth trumpet introduces hideous, demon-like creatures, such as scorpions and locusts, out of the bottomless pit. Although they are not able to kill men,

they torture them so badly that they "will seek death and will not find it."

(16) Revelation 9:13: The sixth trumpet introduces two hundred million horsemen (demon spirit–like death angels), who kill one third of the people. This will occur between the fortieth and forty-second month of the first part of the Tribulation, which brings to 50 percent the amount of the population that is destroyed by God before the midpoint of the Tribulation. These individuals have taken the mark of the Beast and are considered incorrigibles. Since estimates of upward of a quarter of those living at that time will still be saved under the preaching of the 144,000 mentioned in Revelation 7:4, it is possible that 75 percent of the population, 25 percent by martyrdom, will have been destroyed during the first half of the Tribulation period.

Now do you understand that even a mid-Tribulation view of Christ's coming for His Church would mean enormous suffering to millions of believers?

It seems much more reasonable, particularly in the light of His promises for God to save His Church from the "wrath to come," that He would save His Church from the "hour of trial which shall come upon the whole world." That would certainly be characteristic of our loving, merciful, forgiving heavenly Father and Bridegroom. The saints who are martyred during the Tribulation are not part of the Church. They are defined in Revelation 7:14 (NKJV) as "the ones who come out of the great tribulation, and [have] washed their robes and made them white in the blood of the Lamb."

(17) Revelation 11:3–14: The Two Witnesses prophesy for 1,260 days—a ministry, which, if taken literally, would correspond with the forty-two months of judgments already described.

Obviously, these two witnesses are real people with miraculous powers like Moses and Elijah, here to preach and witness during the entire first half of the Tribulation. It may be through their witness that the 144,000 are saved and sent out preaching. As dreadful a time as this will be, God is faithful to provide plenty of Gospel preaching to the nations.

(18) Revelation 11:15: The seventh trumpet judgment introduces the awesome events described in chapters 12–18 and the most severe set of judgments yet reported, the Vial Judgments.

(19) Revelation 17:1–18: This passage describes the destruction of the Babylon-like, false religious system—the great harlot—which will merge all the religions of the world during the first part of the Tribulation (which will take place easily after the Church is raptured). This system will be so powerful that it will dominate both the Antichrist ("the beast") and the ten kings at that time. But because of their hatred for the harlot, at the midpoint of the Tribulation, they will make war on her and kill her.

(20) Revelation 13:1–3: While in the process of killing the harlot, Mystery Babylon, the false religious system, somehow the Antichrist is killed, receiving "a deadly wound," but the wound is miraculously healed. In chapter 12, Satan himself is cast out of heaven, where he has been "the accuser of our brethren," and now he enters the Antichrist's body and resurrects him to a new and even more vicious life.

(21) Revelation 13:4–10: The Antichrist, now incarnated, will force the remaining people of the earth to worship him, except for those whose names are in the Lamb's Book of Life (*see* 2 Thessalonians 2:8–10).

(22) Revelation 13:11–18. The False Prophet will replace the slain religious system, forcing people to worship Antichrist and his image or be killed. Everyone will be compelled to display a "666" mark in order to hold a job and "buy and sell."

Plainly, if the Xhurch were to go through the Tribulation, she would not survive it. And I find no scriptural evidence that any believers will remain at the end of the Tribulation to be raptured, if that event is post-Trib. Remember, the worst half of the Tribulation period, which our Lord termed the "Great Tribulation," has not yet begun! That last forty-two month period is covered by the Vial Judgments.

(23) Revelation 16:1–2: The first vial causes giant sores on those who rejected Christ and instead accepted the mark of the Beast, signifying their worship of him.

(24) Revelation 16:3: The second vial is poured out on the sea, turning it to "blood as of a dead man; and every living creature in the sea died" (NKJV).

(25) Revelation 16:4: The third vial turns the rivers and other sources of water to blood (an especially just judgment, because the people remaining had killed so many Tribulation saints).

(26) Revelation 16:8–9: The fourth vial will intensify the sun's heat until ungodly men blaspheme the name of God.

(27) Revelation 16:10-11: The fifth vial will cause darkness to cover the throne of Antichrist and his entire kingdom. The sores will continue unrelentingly, producing such agony that men will gnaw their tongues for pain, blaspheme God, and refuse to repent.

(28) Revelation 16:13-16: The sixth vial sends lying demon spirits out to the kings of the whole world to bring them down to "the battle of that great day of God Almighty" (NKJV), more popularly known as the Battle of Armageddon.

(29) Revelation 16:17-21: The seventh vial results in a judgment of Almighty God that destroys the entire world system and judges all unsaved men severely. But even though enormous hailstones fall, the unregenerate still refuse to repent. This judgment is so devastating that it prepares the world for the coming of Christ to set up His earthly Kingdom.

(30) Revelation 18:1-24: The destruction of commercial and governmental Babylon—the New World Order, for which man has yearned ever since his rebellion at Babylon—now occurs, possibly during the seventh vial, since it fits there (verse 19) just before earth's final judgment. It will totally collapse the Antichrist's system and further pave the way for the best event of the Tribulation.

(31) Revelation 19:11-21: We finally witness the glorious appearing of Christ in power and great glory as the King of kings and Lord of lords, to set up His thousand-year reign on this earth.

10

Biblical Principles and Political Policies

I DEBATED WHETHER TO INCLUDE this topic in my book. I believe we do have an obligation to be aware of what is going on in the world around us and ensure we are not condoning or taking part in policies that go against what the Bible says.

Disclosure: If you feel you do not want to engage in these political observations and how I feel they relate to the Bible's teaching, feel free to skip over this chapter. I love how Pastor Jack Hibbs addresses the current times. He says things are not falling apart—they are falling into place according to Bible prophecy.

The policies you support should be measured against the principles of the Bible. We will be judged severely if we accept ungodly principles.

Some may ask how this chapter can help with healing. I have spoken with many people who are distraught by what is going on in the world today. Some are so consumed that they feel complete anger, anxiety, and despair. Learning the truth is part of the healing process. The truth is laid out for us in the Bible. If we discover it and follow what has been written, we will be prepared for all the things we are now seeing and the things that are yet to come. In the Bible, the words *"fear not"* are written 365 times—once for every day of the year.

If you are allowing the circumstances of the world to affect your walk with God in any way other than how the Bible teaches us to be, then you are not following what has been written. We must live by the principles of the Bible. This is the reason I have included this chapter. I also believe we must support policies and political leaders who align closest to those biblical principles—not necessarily the person themselves, but the policies that are aligned with that candidate.

If we are silent and not bold enough to let others know that we will not support programs and policies that go directly against God's instructions, then we fall short of following God, and we fall short of helping others follow God's words and instructions.

I will not shy away from tough topics. If we say nothing, we become complacent, and we will also be held accountable. The majority of Germans were not in support of the Nazi party; unfortunately, they were the silent majority.

We are taught to love our neighbor. Condoning any sinful behavior because of a fear of speaking up is not showing love. What that is showing is a *lack* of love. If I just stand by while someone is believing and supporting something that can have such heavy

BIBLICAL PRINCIPLES AND POLITICAL POLICIES

consequences that it will affect how they spend eternity, to me that is cowardly and cruel.

I also started to realize that it is not religion that is creeping into politics; it is politics that is creeping into our faith, our moral decisions, and our ability to hold on to our beliefs without persecution. We are being told that we must follow policies that go against our biblical beliefs by governmental programs or be punished. We are threatened with the loss of our jobs, being called a "racist," or being forced to take medication that does not align with biblical principles. So, yes! We need to speak up. When the followers of God were asked to worship Baal, they stood strong in their beliefs, to the point of being thrown in a fire or put in lions' cages.

I suggest that you test any political policies against the Bible. If they go against the Bible's teachings, then stay clear of the party that supports those policies.

Below are policies that *do not* align with the Bible, in my opinion and understanding of the Word of God. My answer when people ask me why I don't support such policies that do not align with the Bible is simple. I say, "The Bible says . . ." and then follow that with Scripture. It's not by my own understanding, but it's the words that God left for us to follow. *"My thoughts [are higher] than your thoughts"* (Isaiah 55:8–9 NKJV).

> *"For my thoughts are not your thoughts, neither are your ways my ways," saith the Lord. "For as the heavens are higher than the earth, so are my ways higher that your ways, and my thoughts than your thoughts."*
>
> —Isaiah 55:8–9 KJV

Abortion Up to Birth: Psalm 139:13 (NIV) says, *"For you created my inmost being; you knit me together in my mother's womb."* I know abortion is a very touchy subject. But I also know that on Judgment Day, this will be tough to speak about. I watched my children form in their mother's womb, so it is very clear to me that we will all be held accountable. It is also clear to me that the devil uses a tactic like this to hurt God.

Crazed Push for Transgender Surgery in Children: Let's call this what it really is: the genital mutilation of children. As adults, we are supposed to give guidance to our children. We don't let twelve-year-olds buy whiskey, cigarettes, guns, or lottery tickets, but we allow this? Kids can't drive, but they can choose a life-altering medical procedure before coming of age?

Weakened Military: With a weak military, evil ideologies will spread. We have seen the expansion of wars and terrorist activities in the past years under weak leadership.

Poor Handling of the War in Ukraine: When this war started, we were told many lies. We were told a coalition of countries would stand together and enforce sanctions. It seems no one is even attempting to stop this killing. Government contractors and weapons companies are only getting rich and providing kickbacks. We were told in the Bible to be alert for an increase in deception.

Gender Confusion: We are creating PTSD in our children through gender confusion; this, again, is evil. Pornographic books can be found in grade-school libraries. Drag queen story hours are performed for small children. Indoctrination is taking place in our school systems in the name of "inclusion." It is all a lie! And those of

BIBLICAL PRINCIPLES AND POLITICAL POLICIES

us who do not fall in line and choose to stand against these beliefs are now facing persecution.

Endless Push for LGTQ+ "Rights": This has become an obsession for one political party. Sadly, however, among this group we see one of the highest suicide rates. They are being used! It is our command to love one another, but we are not to condone something that goes against our biblical beliefs and leads to the death of even one of God's children.

Open Borders: An open-border policy is not humane; rather, it is leading to death, slavery, sex trafficking, drug trafficking, the enrichment of cartels, and the ruination of the countries from which these immigrants come. (Fentanyl kills over eighty thousand people per year, by the way.) And this is called "humane"? An open border allows terrorists to enter our country unchecked. Other countries are opening their jails and sending their worst offenders through our open borders, including rapists, gang members, and murderers. This is nothing short of an invasion and evil, and in my opinion, it is purposely being orchestrated for some sick agenda. Allowing an open border should be considered treasonous activity!

Eliminated Freedom of Speech: The American people are being censored. Our posts are being taken down, and the media has become propaganda for one political party. They will ruin you if you speak up too loudly. The new term is *lawfare*, a type of warfare conducted through the so-called justice system. This will soon lead to Christians not being allowed to profess their faith if it is left unchecked.

Eliminated Freedom of Religion: This is happening, and it will get worse if the people in power get their way.

Genital Mutilation of Children: This is so monstrous it is worth repeating! This is so evil. Back when we relied on morals in our nation, we recognized evil practices like this. What happened?

Secular Indoctrination of Children: We see this at all levels of our educational system. It is an orchestrated attempt to lead our children away from family values and Christian beliefs.

Division of God's Children for Political Gain: Division by race, gender, or financial status goes against the teachings of God's Word.

Pushing Homelessness and Encouraging Drug Use: One political party is actively handing out drug needles and providing "shoot-up zones," like in Kensington, Pennsylvania, and many other areas. This is cruel and inhumane treatment of our citizens, who are God's children.

Endless and Numerous Wars: In my opinion, the numerous wars in which the United States is now engaged is simply meant to feed the military industrial complex. Follow the money, it is making its way back to the political parties. Humans are just collateral damage.

Lies about Global Warming: This is now called "climate change." It is truly deceitful, and it is ruining people's lives in the pursuit of gaining and maintaining power.

Lies about "Green Energy": Those in charge are willing to destroy the environment by mining for cobalt, silver, and other materials to create this so-called green energy. They also use slave labor and children to mine these products. Do research on the process.

Push toward a One-World Government: The WHO (World Heath Organization), the World Economic Forum, and other

BIBLICAL PRINCIPLES AND POLITICAL POLICIES

worldwide institutions are agencies that are pushing for a one-world government. This has been written about in the book of Revelation, and it is something Christians need to avoid and in which they should refuse to participate.

Erasing Christian Holidays: The current administration celebrated Easter Sunday as Transgender Visibility Day. No religious symbols are allowed at the White House to celebrate Easter.

Removal of Parental Rights: Doctors can now perform life-altering surgeries and prescribe dangerous drugs to our children in some states without parental consent. This is insane to me.

The policies I listed above *do not come from God*. In our culture today, evil is called good, and good is called evil. I will leave it up to you to figure out where you think policies like this come from. To me, they only come from the evil one himself. We know they are not from God.

Policies Matter

Biblical policies with a strong moral grounding are what will keep us closer to God. What we support also matters. We should always check to make sure we are aligned with biblical principles. We also need to trust in God and know that *He's Got Our Six*.

11

Put in the Work

ARE YOU READY TO BEGIN your journey to peace and contentment? I hope you have recited, prayed, and meant the prayer below, also provided at the beginning of the book. If you have not, please take the time to truly reach out to God for healing, contentment, peace, and salvation. God knows your heart. It's not enough to simply say the words. They must come from your heart. I firmly believe that if you put in the work, true healing will then begin.

The Prayer of Salvation

Dear Lord,

I admit that I am a sinner. I have done many things that don't please You. I have lived my life for myself only. I am sorry, and I repent. I ask You to forgive me. I accept You as my Lord and Savior. I believe that Jesus died on the cross for me, to save me. Jesus did what I could not do for myself. I come to You now and ask You to take control of my life; I give it to You. From this day forward, help me to live every day for You in a way that pleases You.

I love You, Lord, and I thank You for the opportunity to spend all eternity with You. Amen.

Just because you have given your life to Christ, that doesn't mean everything will be easy in your life moving forward. In fact, it may get more difficult. The difference is that you will now have God and Jesus helping you through every situation. Please remember this next verse:

Jesus said, "I have told you these things, so that in me you may have peace. In this world you will have trouble. But take heart! I have overcome the world."

—John 16:33 NIV, emphasis mine

God bless you!

LET THE WORK BEGIN!

The Daily Routine

SO, ARE YOU READY TO feel better? Are you ready for God to guide you? Are you ready to put in the work? Let's get started! (I recommend you also visit www.hesgotyoursix.com for additional videos and training guides.)

Six Ways to Get Started

1. First, you must believe, then you must invite God into your life. Commit your life to following Jesus each day the best you know how, for the rest of your life.

- James 4:7–8 (NLT) says, *"So humble yourselves before God. Resist the devil, and he will flee from you. Come close to God, and God will come close to you."*

- God gave us free will. So, now we have to take the first step. Once we submit to God's will, He will honor His promises.

2. Pray.

- Go to a private space every day and pray—even if it's just for a minute. Reach out to God. Create a habit!

3. Read the Bible. Study and apply the Word of God.

- Start reading the Bible every morning. Even if it's to read just one verse, open the Bible, and ask God for understanding! I suggest reading the gospel of John and the book of James for a great start.
- Download the <u>Bible App</u> and listen to the verse of the day.
- Take a forty-day challenge on the Bible App.

4. Attend a Bible-teaching church.

5. Join a small group or Bible study.

- We are all in different ages and stages of our journey with Jesus, but we are not meant to go into battle alone. Get a group that you will commit to being open and honest with. This is key to growth and learning how to combat the attacks of the enemy.

6. Change the things you watch and listen to.

- Garbage In = Garbage Out.
- Limit social media and change what you are subscribing to.
- Watch *The Case for Christ*. This movie is based on a true story. Knowing the facts of the resurrection will lead you to greater faith and the ability to share your beliefs.

- Download The Chosen App or stream it and start watching. This brings Jesus' story to life. This is a good start. Also begin looking for programs, podcasts, and videos that will add spiritual depth to your life.

HGY6 Challenge (Boot Camp with God!)

Let's continue to change our lives.

Only God can heal you, but you must seek Him out. HGY6 is here to give you resources to guide and help you maintain your walk with God. If you are willing to take the steps, work hard, and stay committed to seeking God's help, He promises us He will never leave us.

Do you have a plan to connect with God each day? Only you can change your life!

Challenge #1

Read God's Word (the Bible) and pray every day. Try this for the next forty days, and your life will change. Then keep it up!

1. Get up and find a quiet place.
2. Give God the first of your day, the best of your time. This is what He has asked of us. When you wake up, just talk to God. Thank Him and ask Him to guide your day.
3. Read at least one passage in the Bible. Start with the gospel of John.

4. If you want maximum impact in your life, repeat the steps above before you go to bed. (Thank God for your day, then read the Bible and pray.)

Challenge #2

Change what you put in your body and soul. (Good in = good out.) Would you start a big workout plan, then leave and go and put a bunch of garbage in your body? Not if you were serious about your physical health.

1. Make it a habit to listen to sermons or a worship music radio station.
2. Change your environment! Do not hang out and listen to people who are negative, gossip, put others down, or use foul language. It is hard, but you may just need to walk away and remove yourself from those situations and people. You can be bold and let them know politely and with grace that you would rather talk about something else, and that foul language is something you are trying not to use, so they could help you out by not using it in your conversations.
3. What do your eyes look at every day? Do you guard what you see on your computer, TV, and phone? If not, start now.
4. Turn away from sinful behavior and seek God during times of temptation. God will have your back if you seek Him.
5. What do you watch on TV? What you feed your body will influence your behavior. Good in = good out! If you are allowing filth to infiltrate your spirit, it will take root and fester. I realized that once I had committed myself to Jesus

Christ, He had filled me with the Holy Spirit—the Spirit of God. Would I look at trash on my phone, my computer, or the TV if I were sitting next to God? Well, I am sitting with Him! God's Spirit is *in me*. Whatever I am watching, the Holy Spirit in me is watching, as well, because He is right there with me.

Challenge #3

Change your actions! Live by example. Actions speak louder than words!

1. Begin to show grace and mercy to others even if they do not deserve it, just as God does for you.
2. Increase your patience with others. God has been very patient with you.
3. Pray before each meal, thanking God for the blessings He gives you.
4. Help someone with no expectation of anything in return.
5. Be nice to others. Jesus shared with us the two greatest commandments: love the Lord your God and love others.

Challenge #4

Join a small group.

1. Find one or start one.
2. Having people with whom you can be open about your struggles and hardships in life is a key to maintaining and strengthening your relationship with God.

Challenge #5

Join a church or find one online. YouTube has many pastors you can follow. Below are some suggestions to get you started:

1. Don't buy in to what others say about church, or even your own bad past experience, as an excuse not to attend.
2. Church is just one part of your walk with God.
3. We are all sinners; churchgoers are not exempt from this stipulation.
4. The devil wants nothing more than for you to stay disconnected.

Online church suggestions: Pastor Jack Hibbs, Calvary Chapel, Jupiter Farms; Pastor Allan Jackson; Pastor Robby Gallatry of Long Hollow Church

Challenge #6

Ask someone in need if you can pray for them—right there and then. Put your hand on their shoulder and say a prayer. It doesn't have to be long or eloquent, but it should come from the heart.

Next Steps (Intensive Training)

This next section I call *IT* (Intensive Training), or mashing, as they say in boot camp.

It's time to take your training and dedication to the next level: "God uses ordinary people to do extraordinary things" (*author unknown*).

Find a verse you can read when evil is attacking you.

The attacks will come, but the difference now is that you will know the tactics and you will be prepared and guarded by God. My verse was and still is Philippians 4:13: *"I can do all things through Christ who strengthens me"* (NKJV). Every time I have felt the attack of the enemy, I would recite this verse, either in my mind or out loud. The devil has had a hold on you for many years, and he's not going to give up that easily. This is just part of the armor!

To begin deeper training, you now must turn from whatever has a hold on you. Turn from sin and acknowledge that you are a new creation in Christ. You are no longer of the flesh. When you were born into this world, you were born of the flesh. Once you have accepted Jesus Christ as your Lord and Savior, you are born again, born of the Spirit! You are no longer a citizen of this fallen world. You are a citizen of heaven, God's Kingdom. Heaven will be our home after we die; it is where we will live again.

This reality took some time for me to fully comprehend. These are not my words, but they are the words in the Bible that were given to Paul, an apostle of Christ. I would greatly suggest studying the entire book of Ephesians until you have a full understanding of these words.

> *As for you, you were dead in your transgressions and sins, in which you used to live when you followed the ways of this world and of the ruler of the kingdom of the air, the spirit who is now at work in those that are disobedient. All of us also lived among them at one time, gratifying the cravings of our flesh and following its desires and thoughts. Like the rest, we were by nature deserving of wrath. But because of his great love for us, God, who is rich in mercy, made us alive with Christ even when we were dead in transgressions—it is by grace you have been saved.*
>
> —Ephesians 2:1–5 NIV

Next-Level Training

Challenge #1

Memorize Scripture. Get some 3X5 index cards and then write a verse on one side and the content of that verse on the opposite side.

Week One: Pick one verse and study it every day, first thing in the morning, and then again before you go to bed. Below are two sample verses. Feel free to use one to get started. Or you can pick up your Bible, pray and ask God to help you find a verse, and then use the one He shows you. Finding the verses yourself is part of the training, moving on from here.

"Love the Lord your God with all your heart and with all your soul and with all your mind and with all your strength."

—Mark 12:30 NIV

Submit yourselves, then, to God. Resist the devil, and he will flee from you.

—James 4:8 NIV

Week Two: Add another verse each week for six additional weeks. You will then start to form a habit. God will help you find the verses you need if you simply ask.

Challenge #2

Download a Bible study. Pick a study of one of the four gospels—Matthew, Mark, Luke, or John—and complete the study. You can start this as you are memorizing Scripture. The Bible App has many free studies to choose from. Download the Bible App Now—100% Free.

Continue your studies after you have completed your first. This is an ongoing process of staying close to God and being in relationship with Jesus.

Challenge #3

Watch all four seasons of *The Chosen*. This series brings the Bible to life and will make what you are reading easier to understand. It also changes what you are watching. *The Chosen* has an app, or you can find it on YouTube and most streaming services.

Challenge #4

Ask someone if you can pray for them in person. The next time you encounter someone who is struggling, don't back away from the opportunity God is giving you to help someone else. Put your hand on their shoulder and pray a simple prayer that addresses their situation. Remember that God uses ordinary people to spread His Word.

Challenge #5

Share your story. Our testimony is the most impactful message we have to help others realize we all go through troubles. It's not to compare, but if you have a story memorized about how you came to Christ, your experience of the Holy Spirit, or your transformation, it could be just what someone needs to hear.

I was told to write out my story on paper—keep it short, but to the point, and get comfortable sharing it with others. It might just save their lives.

Challenge #6

If you haven't already been baptized as an adult of your own free will, I suggest you do so. This is such an important step. Baptism is a public acknowledgment of your faith and how you have turned your life over to God. Accepting His will for your life and not relying on your own will is being born again—not from the flesh of our mother, but from the Spirit. Being baptized as a child is good, but you did not personally make that surrender to God and accept the Holy Spirit. This needs to be something you do on your own accord.

Below are a few prayers I like to say. I also repeat the "Our Father" (the "Lord's Prayer"), not just reciting it from memory, but from the heart, as if in a conversation with God.

- *Our Father who art in heaven,*
  hallowed be thy name.
  Thy kingdom come.
  Thy will be done on earth as it is in heaven.
  Give us this day our daily bread,
  And forgive us our trespasses,
  As we forgive those who trespass against us,
  And lead us not into temptation,
  But deliver us from evil. Amen

As your walk with Christ grows, you will be able to add more prayers that speak to you, just as these spoke to me.

- God, when I am weak, You are strong. When I am lonely, You are my Comforter. When I feel unable to keep moving forward, You give me the strength I need to persevere. Please remind me when I feel overwhelmed that You are with me. Refresh my soul and give me rest. In Jesus' name, amen.

- Father God, thank You for giving me Your Word. Scripture is brimming with truth and life, and I never want to take that for granted. I know that I am easily distracted, but I also know that You give me the strength to persevere. Show me how to meditate on Your Word so that I don't disobey You. Teach me to prioritize my relationship with You above everything else. In Jesus' name, amen.

- Jesus, make me more like You. Please remove any behaviors or thought patterns that don't reflect Your character or Your heart for people. Make me bold, brave, and courageous—but keep me humble, kind, and gentle. Let the way I live reflect Your hope and love. And when the opportunity arises, help me to share my faith with genuine joy. Amen.

Congratulations! If you have completed these routines, you are well on your way to a personal relationship with our true Father. God bless you!

ABOUT THE AUTHOR

JOHN GALANTI ROSE FROM A background that wasn't easy, like so many others. John is a proud Navy Veteran and is grateful for the love of his family and God's grace.

Through all the good times and the bad times John always had this feeling that there was something missing.

Once finding God, surrendering himself and making a commitment to a daily routine in the word, John began to understand what it was to have true contentment in all situations.

You may also go to www.hesgotyoursix.com
for videos and ongoing training.

www.ingramcontent.com/pod-product-compliance
Lightning Source LLC
Chambersburg PA
CBHW072159070526
44585CB00015B/1221